HOW 2

A handbook for office workers

second edition

James L. Clark
Chairman, Business Department
Pasadena City College

Lyn R. Clark
Professor, Office Administration Department
Los Angeles Pierce College

Wadsworth Publishing Company
A Division of Wadsworth, Inc.
Belmont, California

Business Editor: Jack B. Rochester
Production Editor: Anne D. Kelly
Cover Design: Cynthia Bassett

Printed in the United States of
America
1 2 3 4 5 6 7 8 9 10—83 82 81 80 79

Library of Congress Cataloging in
Publication Data
Clark, James Leland, 1929–
     How 2: A handbook for office
     workers.

     Published in 1975 under title: How.
     Includes index.
     1. Commercial correspondence—
Handbooks, manuals, etc.
I. Clark, Lyn, joint author.   II. Title.
HF5726.C55 1979   651.7'402
78-24277
ISBN 0–534–00635–3

pReFACE

HOW 2: A Handbook for Office Workers, Second Edition, is designed to assist business students and office personnel by answering the mechanical and format questions and problems connected with typing, transcribing, writing, and mailing business letters and reports. The primary function of *HOW 2* is to act as a reference book. It may also be used, however, as a supplementary classroom learning activity for potential word processors, secretaries, and typists. By using materials provided in the supplementary materials and teaching aids, the instructor may reinforce the principles presented in this handbook.

Special Features

To increase the functional use of *HOW 2* as a reference handbook, several special features, in addition to the table of contents and the index, are included:

1. *Chapter indexers*—edge-of-page printed tabulators so that major sections may be located quickly
2. *Solution Finders*—comprehensive topic indexes at the beginning of each chapter so that solutions to problems may be found easily
3. *Example headings*—italic headings that differentiate aspects of each rule so that specific applications can be isolated
4. *Two-color format*—rules are printed in red and examples are printed in black for ease in locating, reading, and understanding
5. *Spiral binding*—a lie-flat feature so that office personnel may readily compare their problems with the examples

Organization

HOW 2 is organized to deal with two major problem areas concerned with written office communications—mechanical problems and operational problems. Mechanical problems are covered in chapters concerned with punctuation, hyphenation and division of words, capitalization, numbers, abbreviations and contractions, literary and artistic titles, words often misused and confused, grammar, address format, and forms of address.

Operational problems are covered in chapters concerned with letter and memorandum format, reports and manuscripts, mail, telegrams, and cablegrams, and in the appendix on secretarial shortcuts.

Finding Solutions to Problems

Information you need may be located easily and quickly in *HOW 2* by using a four-step process:

1. Find the chapter you need by turning to the list of contents shown on the *outside back cover.*
2. Turn to the Solution Finder at the beginning of that chapter by using the tabs that appear on the outside edge of the pages.
3. Locate the information you need in the Solution Finder. Each main topic is listed alphabetically followed by subsections of that topic and their rule numbers.
4. Turn to the appropriate section within the chapter by referring to the page guide references (the rule numbers shown at the top right corner of the odd-numbered pages).

If information cannot be located through surveying the contents listed on the back cover, use the comprehensive index at the end of the book to find the appropriate section. Then use the tabs on the outside edge of the pages to locate the appropriate chapter and the page guides to find the specific section.

Our Gratitude

Our appreciation and thanks are given to the following people: Dorothy A. Anderson, Foothill College; Robert Blackman, Trend Business Colleges; Mildred Butterfield, Mt. Hood Community College; Juanita Caldwell, Tallahassee Community College; Marjory Q. Clark, Los Angeles Pierce College; Helen A. Crawford, Long Beach City College; Marion E. Graff, California State University, Los Angeles; Ethylmae Hanson, Portland Community College; James Harper, San Jose State University; Mary Jacks, Arizona State University, Tempe; Dolores Kilcherstein, Texas Technical University; Joel Lerner, Sullivan County Community College; L. Jolene Mack, Golden West College; Carol L. McGuire, SUNY Agriculture and Technical College; May Oka, Mt. Hood Community College; Nancy O'Rourke, Mt. Hood Community College; Albert N. Pauls, Fresno City College; Louis S. Pecora, Golden West College; Devern J. Perry, Brigham Young University; Joseph E. Scott, Grays Harbor College; Louise A. Spivey, Golden West College; and Jane M. Thompson, Solano Valley College.

CONTENTS

1
PUNCTUATION

1   Punctuation Solution Finder

1 Comma

1–1. Series

a. In a sentence containing three or more equally ranked elements (words, phrases, or short clauses), place a comma after each item as well as before the conjunction (*and, or, nor*). (See 1–1d for exception to this rule.)

words

Our branch office advertised for an accountant, a secretary, and a clerk-typist.

phrases

Two new employees were hired to supervise office services, improve the filing system, and conduct studies of office procedures.

short clauses

Yesterday I signed the contract, Karen Jones mailed it, and Ralph Harris initiated computer installation procedures.

b. Commas are not used when items in a series are all joined by conjunctions.

words

Neither jewelry *nor* cash *nor* appliances were stolen from the store.

phrases

For several years we have employed custodians to clean the building *and* gardeners to maintain the grounds *and* special crews to perform painting and electrical maintenance.

c. Although generally avoided, *etc.* is sometimes used to indicate "and so forth" at the end of a series. If it is used, *etc.* is set off by commas; it is never preceded by the word *and.*

within a sentence

Staples, paper clips, fasteners, rubber bands, etc., were placed on our last supplies order.

end of sentence

We plan to visit all our branch offices this year--New York, Los Angeles, San Francisco, Chicago, etc.

d. A comma is not used before an ampersand (&) in an organizational name unless the organization officially uses the comma in its name.

no comma

Her first interview is with Gates, Hamilton & Gates.

4

comma

1

Augner, Haight, Liggett, & Phelan is a new accounting firm in the Chicago area.

1–2. Parenthetical Expressions

a. Transitional words and phrases that are considered unnecessary for the grammatical completeness of a sentence and that *interrupt its natural flow* are set off with commas. A partial list of such parenthetical expressions follows:

according to our records	hence	no doubt
accordingly	however	obviously
after all	in addition	of course
all in all	incidentally	on the contrary
all things considered	in conclusion	on the other hand
also	indeed	on the whole
as a matter of fact	in fact	otherwise
as a result	in general	periodically
as a rule	in my opinion	secondly
at any rate	in other words	so
at the same time	instead	that is
besides	in summary	then
between you and me	in the first place	therefore
by the way	in the meantime	thus
consequently	likewise	too
even so	moreover	under the circumstances
finally	namely	unfortunately
for example	needless to say	what is more
fortunately	nevertheless	without a doubt
furthermore	no	yes

beginning of sentence

Needless to say, he is planning to attend the meeting.

end of sentence

The store will be closed over the Labor Day weekend, *without a doubt.*

within a sentence

A large crowd, *nevertheless,* attended the exhibit.

b. Sometimes words and phrases used as parenthetical expressions *do not* interrupt the flow of a sentence. In such cases no commas are used with the expression.

beginning of sentence

Perhaps the package will arrive in Los Angeles by Monday.

end of sentence

My boss is planning a trip to New York *too.*

1

within a sentence

She was *indeed* concerned about the omissions in the financial analysis.

c. Exclamations at the beginning of a sentence are parenthetical expressions that require a comma.

Oh, what a surprise to see Mrs. Hilton at the Christmas party!

Ah, it will not be easy to transfer these holdings into liquid assets!

d. Enumerations or explanations used as parenthetical expressions within a sentence are set off by commas, dashes, or parentheses. Use commas when the enumerated or explanatory information has no internal commas; use dashes or parentheses when the information contains a comma within it or when the information is not closely related to the rest of the sentence.

commas

Only one company, *namely, Consolidated Enterprises,* bid on the contract.

dashes

He had invited several relatives--*namely, Aunt Meredith, Cousin Elma, and Uncle Ben*--to attend the company picnic.

parentheses

Our new vice-president toured several cities *(Cleveland, Columbus, and Toledo)* to find a suitable plant site.

e. A parenthetical expression introducing an enumeration or explanation after a complete thought may be set off with either commas or a semicolon and a comma. If the enumeration or explanation itself is a complete thought or contains internal commas, use a semicolon and a comma. Otherwise, use just commas.

commas

We are expecting two exceptionally large orders next week, *namely,* from Reeds Department Store and Payco.

There are several ways we can cut our expenses during the next quarter, *for example,* by reducing our advertising budget.

semicolon and comma

This customer ordered new furniture for her living room; *namely,* a sofa, two chairs, and a cocktail table.

Your insurance does not cover all hazards; *i.e.,* any losses resulting from earthquake damage are not recoverable.

f. Introductory prepositional phrases essential to the meaning of the sentence should not be mistaken for parenthetical expressions. These phrases answer specifically questions such as when, where, why, or how. Introductory prepositional phrases containing fewer than five words (but not containing a verb form) flow smoothly into the sentence and are *not* followed by a comma.

when?

In the future please place your order with our Eastern Washington office.

At your convenience please return the enclosed form.

where?

At the conference we met agents from two of our other branch offices.

In this case we are unable to grant a full refund of the purchase price.

how?

In this way you will be able to cut your travel costs by 20 percent.

On your own you can prepare for this difficult examination.

why?

For that reason we have turned your account over to our attorney for collection.

On this basis we are unable to employ any additional personnel.

g.   Parenthetical expressions used as adverbs do not require commas.

However brilliant his work may be, Mr. Rogers will not be promoted unless his disposition improves.

Obviously concerned with Ms. Jones's illness, the supervisor phoned her home.

Too many managers were absent yesterday.

1-3.   Direct Address

Nouns of direct address are set off by commas.

beginning of sentence

Ladies and gentlemen, it is a pleasure to address you this evening.

within a sentence

Will you please, *Mr. Jones,* send us your check for $50 by March 30.

end of sentence

You are certainly a competent secretary, *Ms. Boyer.*

1-4.   Appositives

a.   Appositives explain or rename previously mentioned nouns and are usually set off by commas.

1

within a sentence

All the reports were submitted to Mr. Hartford, *our sales manager,* for approval.

end of sentence

She had reservations on the 5:30 p.m. flight, *the last flight to San Francisco that day.*

b. Appositives that are *needed to identify* the person or thing explained or re-named (restrictive appositives) are not set off by commas.

necessary for identification

The book *Secretarial Shortcuts* will be released next week.

Your student *Larry Green* has an appointment to see you tomorrow.

unnecessary for identification

His latest book, *College English,* was released last December.

Your best student, *Ann Freeman,* has an appointment to see you next week.

c. One-word appositives or those forming parts of proper names do not require commas.

one-word appositives

My sister *Ellen* has the leading role in the school play.

I *myself* plan to attend the organizational meeting in Memphis.

proper name

The novel dealt with the life of *Richard the Lionhearted.*

d. Abbreviations appearing after individual or company names and college de-grees written after individual names are set off by commas. *Ltd.* and *Inc.* are set off with commas unless the official company name omits them.

abbreviations after names

Mr. Lowell T. Harrison, *Jr.,* has just been promoted to executive vice-president.

Our firm will be represented by Alan Moskley, *Esq.**

Hargrave & Lyons, *Inc.,* was awarded the equipment contract.

college degree after name of individual

Caroline R. Ryan, *Ph.D.,* is the author of <u>Executive Decision Making</u>.

omission of commas around Inc. or Ltd.

Clothiers *Ltd.* is one of the largest jobbers on the West Coast.

---

*Mr. is never used with the term *Esq.*

e. Words or expressions referred to simply as words or expressions should be underscored or placed in quotation marks rather than set off by commas.

underscored

The word <u>convenience</u> is often misspelled in business letters.

quotation marks

The phrase "Thanking you in advance" is an outdated expression that should be avoided in business letters.

1–5. Dates and Time Zones

a. Dates containing combinations of weekday, calendar date, and year require commas; commas are not used with a calendar date expressed alone.

calendar date expressed alone

On *February 28* our books were audited by the Internal Revenue Service.

calendar date and year

On *February 28, 1979,* our books were audited by the Internal Revenue Service.

weekday and calendar date

On *Tuesday, February 28,* our books were audited by the Internal Revenue Service.

weekday, calendar date, and year

On *Tuesday, February 28, 1979,* our books were audited by the Internal Revenue Service.

b. Expressions of month and year may be written with or without commas as long as consistency is maintained.

with commas

In *March, 1981,* we will release our new line of products.

without commas

In *March 1981* we will release our new line of products.

c. Set off by commas any time zones used with clock times.

Our flight will leave Denver at 9:35 a.m., *MST,* and arrive in New York at 3:18 p.m., *EST.*

1–6. Addresses

a. Elements within an address are separated by commas.

1

name and complete address

Please send the check to *Ms. Harriet Buckley, 14832 Ventura Boulevard, Encino, California 91316.*

complete address only

Mr. Livingston may be reached at *740 Gayley Avenue, Los Angeles, California 90025.*

b. Use commas to set off a state following the name of a city.

within a sentence

The letter was sent to Kansas City, *Missouri,* in error.

end of sentence

On our tour we will visit Boston, *Massachusetts.*

1–7. Coordinating Conjunctions

a. Place a comma before a coordinating conjunction (*and, but, or, nor*) that separates two independent clauses in a compound sentence. No comma is used if both clauses are not totally independent and could not stand alone as separate sentences. (See 1–18 for use of semicolon instead of comma.)

two independent clauses

Several salespeople will reach their goals this month, and they will earn a bonus trip to Philadelphia.

There are still 43 orders to fill, but we will close for vacation as scheduled.

I have not purchased any new appliances within the past month, nor have I purchased any new furniture from your store.

no second independent clause

I hope to complete this project by Wednesday but cannot mail it to the district office until Friday.

We are aware that sales have increased in your district and that another salesperson should be assigned to your territory.

b. In imperative sentences the subject *you* is understood. Separate with a comma two independent clauses, regardless if either one or both are in the imperative form.

Ship the books to me at Eastern High School, but send the bill to the bookstore manager of Grant High School.

Please call Dr. Greenberg's office tomorrow morning, and his nurse will let you know what time the doctor is expected to finish surgery.

c. When a simple adverb, introductory phrase, or dependent clause precedes two clauses, these clauses are not independent. Consequently, no comma is used between them.

simple adverb

Please call the doctor's office tomorrow morning and arrange to have your appointment changed to next week. (The adverb *please* modifies both *call* and *arrange.* Therefore, the two clauses are not independent of each other and no comma is used.)

introductory phrase

During the next month the board will visit several sites in Memphis and they will make a decision regarding the location of the new branch office. (*During the next month* applies equally to both clauses. Consequently, they are not independent and are not separated by a comma.)

dependent clauses

If Mr. Howard calls, ask him for his address and send the brochure to him. (Subject *you* is understood in both clauses. *If Mr. Howard calls* applies to both clauses. Therefore, they are not independent and no punctuation mark is used.)

As soon as we receive your response, we can notify our distributor and he will ship your order immediately. (In this case *As soon as we receive your response* applies to both clauses; therefore, no punctuation mark is needed between the last two clauses.)

d.   Omit the comma in very short compound sentences connected by *and.*

Sharpen the pencils and return them immediately.

Do it now and you will be rewarded.

She demonstrated and we watched.

1–8. Two or More Adjectives

Use commas to separate two or more independent adjectives that modify a noun. No commas are needed, though, when the first adjective modifies the second adjective and the noun as a unit. To identify independent adjectives (1) reverse the adjectives, (2) read the adjectives independently, and (3) read the sentence with the word *and* between the adjectives. If the sentence makes sense with the adjectives read in these ways, then commas should be placed between them.

independent adjectives

He enclosed a *stamped, addressed* envelope.

The president had surrounded herself with *efficient, intelligent* assistants.

We received a *long, demanding, discourteous* letter from your company.

1

first adjective modifies second adjective and noun

The posters were lettered in *large bold* print.

He received several *attractive business* offers.

1–9. Introductory Clauses

a. An introductory dependent clause is separated from the rest of the sentence by a comma. Dependent clauses contain a subject and a verb and usually begin with one of the words listed below.

as	after	provided	until
if } are most common	although	since	whenever
when	because	so	while
	before	unless	

When Mr. Jones inherited $10,000, he invested the money in mutual funds.

So that we may reach a decision by March 14, please submit the papers immediately.

b. A shortened form of an introductory clause is separated from the rest of the sentence by a comma.

If so, the delivery of these materials will be delayed. (If that is so, ...)

As agreed, he will be dismissed. (As we have agreed, ...)

Whatever the reason, I would like to have the error corrected immediately. (Whatever the reason may be, ...)

c. Occasionally an introductory clause may be preceded by an introductory expression. In these cases place a comma only after the introductory clause.

Mrs. Jones said that *when this account is paid,* we will revoke their credit privileges.

I hope that *before you file your income tax return,* you will check with our tax attorneys on this issue.

d. When an introductory clause is followed by two other clauses, place a comma only after the introductory clause.

When Jerold answers the telephone, he speaks clearly and he answers all questions courteously.

If you wish employment with our company, fill out the enclosed application form and mail it in the enclosed envelope.

1–10. Introductory Phrases

a. An introductory infinitive phrase (a verb preceded by *to*) is followed by a comma.

1

To arrive at an immediate decision, Mr. Holmes called a meeting of the stockholders.

To carry out the original plans, Miss Hyde hired two additional employees.

b. An introductory participial phrase (a verb form used as an adjective) is followed by a comma.

Hoping to obtain several large orders, Mr. Irwin embarked upon a selective advertising campaign.

Concerned about the sudden decrease in sales, Ms. Alexander flew to the West Coast.

c. An introductory prepositional phrase (a group of words that includes a preposition and an object) is separated from the rest of the sentence by a comma if it contains a verb form *or* five or more words. A partial list of prepositions used to begin introductory prepositional phrases follows:

about	among	behind	during	on	until
above	around	below	for	over	up
after	at	between	from	through	upon
along	before	by	in	under	with

verb form

Upon receiving the papers, Swift & Company filed suit against its former parent company.

five or more words

During the past few days of litigation, concessions were made by both sides.

no verb and fewer than five words

In the magazine article several new medical discoveries were discussed.

d. An introductory phrase that is preceded by an introductory expression is treated as if the introductory expression were not included.

infinitive phrase

Mr. Wilson explained that *to meet our production deadline,* we would have to work overtime the remainder of the week.

participial phrase

Mrs. Winston expressed concern over the poor telephone techniques used by our receptionist; and *speaking clearly and distinctly,* she demonstrated how Miss Davis should handle incoming calls.

prepositional phrase, fewer than five words

We were notified that *on Monday* we will resume our regular schedule.

1

prepositional phrase, five or more words

I hope that *in view of the urgency of the situation,* we will obtain the cooperation of our staff.

e. Any phrase that represents the subject or is part of the predicate is not followed by a comma.

infinitive phrase

To arrive at an immediate decision was Mr. Reed's intent.

participial phrase

Hoping to obtain several large orders is the reason Mr. Irwin agreed to the advertising plan.

prepositional phrase

During the past few days of litigation came several unexpected concessions.

1–11. Restrictive and Nonrestrictive Phrases and Clauses

A restrictive clause or phrase is essential to the meaning of a sentence, and commas are not used. Nonrestrictive clauses or phrases, however, merely add another idea and do not substantially modify the meaning of the sentence. They are not essential, and they do require commas.

a. Relative clauses (those beginning with *who, whose, whom, which,* or *that*) are either restrictive (no comma) or nonrestrictive (comma required).

restrictive and essential to meaning

Office employees *who can type and take shorthand* can obtain well-paying jobs. (Tells which kind of office employees.)

nonrestrictive and not essential to meaning

Ms. Kennedy, *who can type and take shorthand,* can obtain a well-paying job. (Additional idea.)

In the first example the clause "who can type and take shorthand" limits the type of office employees who "can obtain well-paying jobs." In the second example "who can type and take shorthand" is of no assistance in identifying Ms. Kennedy but is merely an additional idea. Therefore, this is a nonrestrictive clause and is set off by commas.

restrictive and essential to meaning

All students *who are enrolled in history classes* will take part in organizing World Affairs Day. (Tells which students.)

nonrestrictive and not essential to meaning

Joseph, *who is enrolled in a history class,* will take part in organizing World Affairs Day. (Additional idea.)

b. Careful writers will use *that* for restrictive clauses (no comma) and *which* for nonrestrictive clauses (comma required).

restrictive

He has written a new book *that will be released next December.*

nonrestrictive

Her new book, *which was scheduled for spring publication,* will be released next December.

c. A dependent clause that follows the main clause may be restrictive (no comma) or nonrestrictive (comma required).

restrictive and essential to meaning

We will ship your order *as soon as your account is approved.* (Tells when.)

The company has doubled its monthly sales *since the advertising campaign started.* (Tells when.)

The company president retired last month *because his doctor recommended a six-month leave of absence.* (Tells why.)

nonrestrictive and not essential to meaning

He has written his letter of resignation, *although I do not believe he will submit it.* (Additional idea.)

She will continue with her plans for introducing a new product, *whatever the competition might be.* (Additional idea.)

Several executives will tour our new South Haven plant, *where we will be hiring several hundred new employees.* (Additional idea.)

d. A dependent clause used parenthetically within a sentence is nonrestrictive and is set off with commas.

Sales figures for last year, *as you can see from the financial reports,* were nearly 10 percent higher than we had projected.

On Tuesday morning, *when you arrive for the meeting,* please give the manuscript to my secretary.

e. Participial, infinitive, or prepositional phrases within a sentence may be restrictive (no comma) or nonrestrictive (comma required).

participial restrictive

All employees *planning to attend the picnic* must sign up by July 1. (Tells who.)

participial nonrestrictive

The entire accounting staff, *planning to attend the picnic,* arranged for car pools. (Additional idea.)

15

1

infinitive restrictive

We are planning *to attend the company picnic* on July 1. (Tells what.)

infinitive nonrestrictive

The picnic will be held on July 4, *to mention only one company social function.* (Additional idea.)

prepositional restrictive

The announcements *for the company picnic* will be ready June 15. (Tells what.)

prepositional nonrestrictive

We are planning, *in response to requests,* an annual company picnic. (Additional idea.)

1–12. Contrasting Expressions

Contrasting, limiting, or opposing expressions are set off with commas. Words often used to introduce these expressions are *not, never, but, seldom,* and *yet.*

contrasting expression

She had considered selling her stocks, *not her real estate,* to increase her liquid assets.

limiting expression

The association will give us four tickets, *but only for members of our sales staff.*

opposing expression

The sooner we are able to contact our investors in Chicago, *the sooner* we will be able to finance this new project.

1–13. Omitted Words

Commas are often used to indicate the omission of words when the context of the sentence makes the omitted words clearly understood.

Four new secretaries were hired in the Accounting Department; three, in the Policy Issue Department. (Three *new secretaries were hired* in the Policy Issue Department.)

Last week Mr. Higgins dictated three complete reports; this week, two complete reports. (This week *Mr. Higgins dictated* two complete reports.)

Our A-100 contract expired on March 10; the A-107 contract, March 23; and the A-116, March 31. (The A-107 contract *expired on* March 23, and the A-116 *contract expired on* March 31.)

1–14. Punctuation for Clarity

a. Two identical verbs that appear together in a sentence are separated by a comma.

Whoever *wins, wins* a trip to Miami.

Whatever *occurs, occurs* with the knowledge of the president.

Whoever *travels, travels* at his own risk.

b. Words repeated for emphasis are separated by a comma.

Many, many years ago this company was founded by Mr. Bernard Harris.

It has been a *long, long* time since one of our vice-presidents visited the West Coast.

c. A word or phrase that could be read incorrectly with the words that follow is set off by a comma.

Ever since, she has been employed by the Hirschell Corporation of Boston.

The week before, the corporation expanded its operations to Brazil.

d. A name written in inverted form is separated by a comma between the last name and the first name.

Irwin, Carl   Luers, Barbara R.

1–15. Short Quotations

a. A short quoted sentence is set off from the rest of the sentence by a comma. When the quoted sentence is broken into two parts, commas are required before and after the interjected thought.

beginning quotation

"All employees will receive two days' vacation after the contract is completed," said Mr. Jones.

interrupted quotation

"All employees will receive two days' vacation," said Mr. Jones, *"after the contract is completed."*

ending quotation

Mr. Jones said, *"All employees will receive two days' vacation after the contract is completed."*

b. Unless the quotation is interrupted, do not use commas when the quoted sentence is a question or an exclamation.

question

"When will the vacation period begin?" asked Ms. Snow.

1

interrupted question

"When," asked Ms. Snow, "will the vacation period begin?"

exclamation

"What a wonderful opportunity you have given our staff!" exclaimed Mr. Stevens.

interrupted exclamation

"What a wonderful opportunity," exclaimed Mr. Stevens, "you have given our staff!"

c. No comma is needed to set off part of a quotation that is woven into a complete sentence or one that is not a complete thought.

woven into sentence

The chairperson operated on the premise that "a stitch in time saves nine."

John is reported to have said that "no one will be able to take a vacation until June."

incomplete sentence

Please mark this package "Fragile."

The personnel manager advised me "to submit my application as soon as possible."

His check was stamped "Insufficient Funds."

d. When a comma and a quotation mark fall at the same point in a sentence, place the comma inside the closing quotation mark. Place a period also inside the closing quotation mark.

"Please arrive at the airport by 9 p.m.," requested Mrs. Chambers.

Her last magazine article, "Western Travel," appeared in the Automotive Digest.

John said, "Be sure to mail your report by June 11."

e. For placement of question marks and exclamation points with closing quotation marks, see 1–44a, b.

1–16. Numerals

a. Numerals of more than three digits require commas.

1,320	1,293,070
51,890	23,092,946
963,481	

b. Two figures appearing consecutively in a sentence are separated by a comma.

Of this *$23,000, $12,000* is secured by real property.

During *1979, $76,000* worth of sales were financed through this plan.

c. Commas are omitted in years, house numbers, zip codes, telephone numbers, decimal fractions, metric measurements, and any word-numeral combinations. In metric measurements, use a space to separate all numerals containing *more than four* digits.

years

1979   1838

house number

9732 Porter Street

zip code

Northridge, CA 91324

telephone number

(213) 482-9768

decimal fraction

.2873

metric measurements

1200 kilometers *(but)* 10 200 kilometers

word-numeral combinations

Serial No. 83621   page 1276   Room 1890

d. Volume numbers and page references are separated by commas.

Please refer to Volume XI, page 9.

The article appeared in Volume X, July 1978, page 23.

e. Measurements (such as weights, capacities, dimensions, etc.) are treated as single elements and are not interrupted by commas.

weight

Their new baby weighed *8 pounds 7 ounces.*

capacity

The recipe required *4 quarts 1 cup* of milk.

time period

Our flight time was estimated to be *2 hours 40 minutes.*

1 Semicolon

1–17. Independent Clauses Without Coordinating Conjunctions

a. A semicolon is used between two or more closely related independent clauses (complete thoughts that could stand alone as separate sentences) that are not connected with a coordinating conjunction *(and, or, but, nor)*.

two independent clauses

Several orders were delayed in the Dallas office last month; Ms. Williams will check into our shipping procedures there.

Plan to attend the next American Management Association meeting; it will benefit you greatly.

three independent clauses

Mr. Horowitz drafted the contract specifications last week; Mr. Aames consulted the firm's attorneys on Monday; Mr. Dotson signed and mailed the company's offer on Wednesday.

b. Short and closely related independent clauses may be separated by commas.

two short independent clauses

She collated, I stapled.

three short independent clauses

The vase teetered, it fell, it broke.

I came, I saw, I conquered.

1–18. Independent Clauses With Coordinating Conjunctions

Two independent clauses linked with a coordinating conjunction are normally separated by a comma. If either or both of the clauses contain one or more commas, however, they should be separated by a semicolon.

no comma within clauses

She planned to attend the Chicago meeting, but several important matters interfered with her plans.

commas in one clause

Several new orders were recently placed through the Miami office; and Ms. Frisby, our merchandising director, was pleased with the progress of this new office.

commas in both clauses

You, of course, need not attend the committee meeting; but I believe it would be helpful, Mr. Plotkin, if you read over the minutes before addressing the board of directors.

1–19. Independent Clauses With Transitional Expressions

Two independent clauses (complete thoughts) separated by a transitional expression require a semicolon. A partial list of common transitional expressions follows. In addition, those expressions listed in 1–2 may be considered transitional expressions when two complete thoughts are closely related.

accordingly	indeed	notwithstanding	still
besides	in fact	on the contrary	then
consequently	in other words	on the other hand	therefore
furthermore	likewise	otherwise	thus
hence	moreover	so	yet
however	nevertheless		

A comma is used after a transitional expression of more than one syllable or where a strong pause is needed after a one-syllable expression.

transitional expression with one syllable

It will be difficult for the library staff to obtain a budget increase; *thus* it will not be possible to order all the books requested.

transitional expression containing more than one syllable

New catalogs will be shipped to our customers the first week in February; *therefore,* we can expect a 20 percent sales increase for the months of February, March, and April.

1–20. Series Containing Commas or Complete Thoughts

a. Items in a series are usually separated by commas. When, however, one or more of the elements contain a comma, use semicolons to separate the items.

Representatives from Boston, Massachusetts; Los Angeles, California; and Denver, Colorado, were not present at the conference.

Among those present at the convention were Mr. Harmon Fieldcrest, president of Fieldcrest Steel Industries; Dr. Garland Hansen, research director for the University of Wisconsin; Mrs. Joyce Morton, vice-president of Wisconsin State Bank; and Ms. Georgia Fillmore, secretary-treasurer of CRA Consultants, Inc.

b. Three or more independent clauses (complete thoughts) comprising a series are separated by semicolons. Only very short clauses are separated by commas.

short clauses

It rained, it hailed, and it snowed during our stay in Philadelphia.

1

long clauses

Nearly 7,000 circulars were mailed to prospective clients in 1972; over 15,000 circulars were mailed in 1977; and next year we plan to mail over 10,000 new brochures as well as 20,000 circulars.

long clauses with commas

Mr. John Harris, our company president, will arrive Saturday; Mrs. Olga Williams, one of our vice-presidents, will arrive Monday; and Ms. Carol Watson, our company treasurer, will arrive Tuesday.

1–21. Enumerations and Explanations

a. When words or phrases that introduce enumerations or explanations follow an independent clause (complete thought), a semicolon or comma is used before the introductory expression and a comma is used after it. If the words following the expression contain commas or form another complete thought, use a semicolon before the expression. If not, use a comma. Some common introductory expressions follow.

as	for instance	that is (i.e.)
for example (e.g.)	namely (viz.)	that is to say

semicolon and comma

Many factors have contributed to the sharp increase in production costs during the last three months; namely, price increases in raw materials, wage increases for electrical workers, and overtime salaries for the entire production staff.

To open its Syracuse office, Caldwell Industries advertised for a number of new employees; that is to say, not all the staff members were willing to transfer to the new location.

commas

You may wish to call Ms. Hendrix for further advice, for example, to inquire which filing system would be more efficient for your office.

b. Enumerations or explanations used as parenthetical expressions within a sentence are not set off by semicolons. Use commas when the enumerated or explanatory information has no internal commas; use dashes or parentheses when the information contains internal punctuation.

commas

Your accounting procedures, *for example, posting customer deposits,* can be streamlined by our new computer system.

dashes

Because of current economic conditions, we must find new vendors for some of our audio-visual equipment--*i.e., cassette tape recorders, video playback units, and carousel projectors*--to stay within our budget allocations.

1

parentheses

Your recommendations *(namely, increasing our staff, improving our hiring procedures, and revamping our testing program)* were approved unanimously by the board.

c. Enumerations or explanations without introductory expressions are not set off by semicolons. Such expressions are preceded by a colon.

Several new items were introduced in this popular line: gloves, scarves, and hosiery.

The following people were present at the sales managers' meeting: Roberta Adams, Horace Brubaker, Philip Haledon, and Susan McCloskey.

1–22. Semicolon Placement

Place the semicolon outside quotation marks and parentheses.

quotation marks

Last month Mr. Harrison promised, "I will mail you a check the first of next month"; yet we have received no money or an explanation from him.

parentheses

Several of our staff from the Accounting Department were out ill (with the flu); consequently, the end-of-the-month reports will be a week late in reaching the home office.

Colon

1–23. Formally Enumerated or Listed Items

a. Use a colon after an independent clause (complete thought) that introduces a formal listing or enumeration of items. Words commonly used for introductory expressions include "the following," "as follows," "these," and "thus." Sometimes, however, the introductory expression is implied rather than stated directly.

In determining whether to use a colon or semicolon for introducing enumerated items, use the colon when the enumeration is not preceded by a transitional introductory expression such as *namely, i.e., for example, that is,* or *e.g.* If an introductory expression immediately precedes the listing, use a semicolon. (See 1–21a for examples.)

direct introduction

Mrs. Robinson ordered *the following* furniture and equipment for her offices: three desks, six chairs, two sofas, two electric typewriters, one electronic calculator, and one adding machine.

1

These rules should be observed for a successful job interview:

1. Dress appropriately.
2. Appear interested in the company and the job.
3. Answer questions courteously.
4. Thank the interviewers for their time.

implied introduction

Several kinds of new typewriters were ordered for the offices: IBM, Olivetti, Olympia, Royal, and Smith-Corona.

b. In three situations the colon is not used to introduce listings of items: (1) when an intervening sentence separates the introductory sentence and the enumerated items, (2) when the enumerated items are introduced by a *being* verb, and (3) when the listing is preceded by a preposition or conjunctive adverb.

no colon: intervening sentence

The following new silverware patterns will be available January 1. They will be introduced to our dealers next month.

Fantasia	Sunburst
Apollo	Moonglow

no colon: listing after being verb

The words most commonly misspelled *were* "convenience," "occasionally," "commodity," "consequently," and "accommodate."

no colon: listing after preposition

Sales meetings are scheduled *for* January 3, February 4, March 7, and April 9.

no colon: listing after conjunctive adverb

Please order some additional supplies; *namely,* bond paper, legal-size envelopes, and shorthand dictation pads.

1–24. Explanatory Sentences

Separate two sentences by a colon when the second sentence explains, illustrates, or supplements the first.

explains

During the next three months, we will gross approximately 50 percent of our annual sales: major toy purchases occur during September, October, and November.

illustrates

Our new advertising campaign will be directed to buyers of economy cars: we will stress gas mileage, maintenance costs, and reliability.

supplements

Several new customers complained about the delay in receiving their charge account plates: they wished to have them in time to complete their holiday shopping.

1–25. Long Quotations

Long one-sentence quotations and quotations of two or more sentences are introduced by a colon.

long one-sentence quotation

Miss Allison Williams, personnel manager of Higgins Corporation, reported: "Graduates from the University of Southern California's School of Business have been placed in a number of our divisions, and they have risen to middle-management positions within a three-year period."

quotation of two or more sentences

One item of importance was noted from the board minutes of November 16:

Two new products, which will revolutionize word processing, will be introduced on July 1. Trade journal publicity and direct-mail advertising will be the major vehicles for distributing information about these products. Efforts by the sales staff for January and February will be directed specifically at marketing the Model AB 1781 and the Model AB 2782 communication networks.

1–26. Special Purpose Uses for Colon

a. In business letters a colon is placed after the salutation when the mixed punctuation format (see 10–19) is used.

Dear Bill: Dear Ms. Corrigan: Gentlemen:

b. Use the colon to separate hours and minutes in expressions of time.

We will arrive at *8:30 a.m.* on Tuesday, March 24.

At *12:15 p.m.* Ms. Hardesty is scheduled to address the Compton Chamber of Commerce.

c. In expressing ratios, use the colon to represent the word *to*.

The label instructions recommend proportions of *4:1*.

The union members voted *2:1* against accepting the new contract.

d. The colon is often used to separate items in literary references.

between place of publication and publisher

Hoffer, Charles R. *The Understanding of Music.* Belmont, California: Wadsworth Publishing Company, Inc., 1978, 483 pp.

between titles and subtitles

William C. Himstreet and Wayne Murlin Baty, *Business Communications: Principles and Methods* (Belmont, California: Wadsworth Publishing Company, Inc., 1977), p. 151.

biblical citations

As an introduction to his sermon, the minister quoted Psalm *23:1.* (Chapter 23, verse 1)

1–27. Colon Placement

a. In *typewritten* copy leave a double space after a colon.

May I please have the following documents by next week: copies of the rental agreement, the returned check, and the 30-day notice to move.

b. Place the colon outside closing quotation marks and parentheses.

closing quotation mark

Several staff members have already read her latest article, "Closing the Sale Effectively": they had received advance copies last week.

closing parenthesis

Several contractors were being considered for the new project (Mountain Hills): Wyeth and Sons, Burnside Developers, and Hartman Associates.

1–28. Capitalization With Colons

a. When a colon is used to introduce a horizontal listing of items, the initial letter after the colon is not capitalized unless it begins a proper noun.

lowercase

Place the following items in the tray: the original invoice, the duplicate invoice, and the shipping copy.

proper noun capitalized

Four employees were promoted last week: Teresa Caruana, Ina Geller, Gary Oliver, and Daniel Streebing.

b. If two sentences are separated by a colon, do not capitalize the first letter of the second sentence when that sentence explains or supplements the first one unless the second sentence begins with a proper noun.

lowercase

Your account has been temporarily closed: outstanding bills for $327 still remain unpaid.

proper noun capitalized

The award for $500 was given to Mary Ellen Guffey: Dr. Guffey's essay was the most original one submitted.

c. Capitalize the first word after a colon when the colon introduces a formal rule or principle stated as a complete sentence.

You should be able to apply the following rule in typing all your business correspondence: Always place commas and periods inside the closing quotation mark.

Mr. Wilson emphasized the importance of strict adherence to the following policy: In case of absence all employees must notify their immediate supervisor by 8:30 a.m. of that day.

d. When two or more sentences follow a colon, capitalize the initial letter of each sentence.

Several suggestions emerged from the discussion: To begin with, an engineering firm should be consulted to determine the extent of damage to the property. Then, a building contractor should be contacted for estimates to repair the damage. Finally, financial institutions should be surveyed to obtain the best terms for reconstructing the property.

e. Capitalize the initial letter of material introduced by short words such as *Note, Attention,* or *For Sale.*

Warning: All cars parked illegally will be towed away at the owner's expense.

Caution: Please hold children by hand.

f. Capitalize the initial word of quoted material that follows a colon.

Mr. Rosen informed the board of expansion plans for this year: "Property has been purchased on the corner of Tampa and Nordhoff at a cost of $80,000. Construction of our new branch office will begin early this spring, and we can plan to open this office in July or August."

Dash

1–29. Parenthetical Elements

a. Parenthetical elements are usually set off from the rest of the sentence by commas. When the parenthetical element contains commas, however, substitute dashes (or parentheses) for the separating commas. Use dashes when the parenthetical element requires emphasis. A dash is formed by typing two hyphens with no space before, between, or after.

Last month Miss Owens--with the hope of increasing sales, recruiting new employees, and establishing sources of supply--made several trips to the East Coast.

1

Three state dignitaries--Governor Hanson Williams, Attorney General Steven Mills, and Secretary Willard Robinson--attended the opening session of the convention.

b. To achieve greater separation, abrupt parenthetical elements or those requiring emphasis may be separated from the rest of the sentence by dashes.

abrupt parenthetical element

Her only concern--notwithstanding her interest in job security--was finding employment in an organization where opportunities for advancement were numerous.

emphatic parenthetical element

Several orders were rerouted to the Milwaukee office--not to the Salt Lake City branch.

c. Dashes may be used to set off a brief summary or appositive from the rest of the sentence.

summary

Thanksgiving, Christmas, and New Year's Day--these are the only holidays on which the store will be closed.

appositive

Additional heavy-duty equipment--bulldozers and graders--was needed to complete the project.

d. For emphasis use a dash in place of a comma or a semicolon to introduce an example or explanation.

example requiring emphasis

Insurance coverage adequate five years ago may no longer fulfill the purpose for which it was designed--for example, if current inflationary trends continue, fire and theft insurance may not cover the replacement cost of the insured properties.

explanation requiring emphasis

Our sales of greeting cards have increased 25 percent since 1977--namely, from $100,000 to $125,000.

e. Afterthoughts or side thoughts generated from the text, but not necessarily part of it, may be separated from the rest of the sentence by dashes.

side thought

All members of our staff were invited to the conference on simplifying communication procedures--only Ms. Harris was unable to attend the session.

afterthought

Mrs. Wilson had planned to finish the correspondence this afternoon--at least John thought she had planned to do it then.

1–30. Hesitations in Verbal Reports

Use dashes to indicate hesitations, falterings, or stammering in reports of conversations, testimonies, or speeches.

Miss Tomlin: Yes, Mr President--we expect perhaps a--oh--35 percent increase in sales during the next year.

Mr Schatz: Well--perhaps a new inventory control system will solve some of the current problems.

1–31. Source of Quotations

A dash is placed before the source of a quotation when the source is listed after the quotation.

"We can expect a great decrease in our unemployment rate during the next ten months."

--H. J. Scott

"The difference between the right word and the almost right word is the difference between lightning and the lightning bug."

--Mark Twain

1–32. Format and Placement of Dash

a. Form the dash by typing consecutively two hyphens; leave no space before, after, or between the hyphens. A dash never begins a new line, but it may appear at the end of a line.

end of line

Contract negotiations--after reaching an impasse on December 20--
were resumed on January 5.

within line

Several influential community organizations--the Kiwanis Club, the Chamber of Commerce, and the Rotary Club--sponsored Mr. Harrison Strong for the vacant seat on the board of education.

b. The only punctuation mark that may precede an opening dash is a period in an abbreviation. Closing dashes may be preceded by a period in an abbreviation, a question mark, or an exclamation point.

opening dash after abbreviation

Prices quoted on all Eastern furniture were f.o.b.--freight charges from Pennsylvania to Los Angeles amounted to $834.

1

closing dash after question mark

A new kind of after-dinner mint--do you know which one I mean?--was introduced by the Wafer Candy Company last month.

Period

1–33. End of Sentence

Place a period at the end of a declarative sentence, an imperative statement or command, an indirect question, and a polite request. Polite requests end with a period even though they may appear to have the format of a question. A polite request (1) asks the reader to perform a specific action and (2) is answered by the reader's compliance or noncompliance with the request.

declarative sentence

Several new products were introduced to the stockholders at the February 5 meeting.

imperative statement

Answer the telephone before the third ring.

indirect question

She asked who would be attending the conference scheduled for next week.

polite request

May I please have your reply by February 4.

Will you please write out your check and mail it in the enclosed envelope by June 4.

1–34. End of Independent Phrase

Independent phrases, those phrases representing implied complete thoughts not directly connected with the following thought, are concluded with a period.

Now, to get to the point. Will you be able to accept the responsibility of conducting a sales campaign during June?

Yes, for the most part. Our salespeople have increased their sales since the new incentive program was initiated.

1–35. Abbreviations and Initials

a. An abbreviation is concluded with a period. After abbreviations for federal agencies and business or government organizations, however, the periods may be omitted.

period after abbreviation

Fletcher, Hagan, Ross and Company, *Inc.,* released several new stock issues.

periods after abbreviations

Mr. Haynes requested that all orders be sent on a *c.o.d.* basis.

no periods with business or government agencies

Hopefully, the educational project director for *NASA* will be able to address our convention.

Did you purchase additional *IBM* stock?

b.   Place a period after an initial.

Ms. Charlene *P.* Holt accepted the invitation to address the convention participants.

We have tried for several days to contact *A. F.* Elliott.

1–36.   Outlines

a.   Use periods after letters and numbers in outlines, except those enclosed in parentheses.

```
I.      . . . . .
        A.      . . . . .
        B.      . . . . .
                1.      . . . .
                2.      . . . .
                        a.      . . . . .
                        b.      . . . . .
                                (1)     . . . . .
                                (2)     . . . . .
                                        (a)     . . . . .
                                        (b)     . . . . .
II.     . . . . .
```

b.   Use periods after complete sentences in outlines and listings. No punctuation mark is placed after an incomplete thought.

periods—complete sentences

A.   Two new processes were developed as a result of the experiments.
    1.   Lamination of fiberglass to wooden surfaces contributes to vessel buoyancy.
    2.   Sealing of surfaces prevents excessive moisture absorption.

no periods—incomplete sentences

A.   New Processes
    1.   Lamination of fiberglass to wooden surfaces
    2.   Sealing of surfaces

1

1–37. Decimals

Periods are used to signify decimals.

It was hard to believe that *34.7* percent of the students failed the final examination.

Last year Mr. Phoenix paid $120 for the 2,000 sales announcements; this year he paid *$145.50* for the same kind and number.

1–38. Emphasis and Omission

An ellipsis, a series of three periods with a space before and after each period, is used for emphasis in advertising material or for showing omissions in quoted material. In showing omissions, indicate the completion of a thought with an additional period immediately after the last word.

emphasis

Place your order today . . . for relief from tension headaches . . . for ending miserable aches and pains . . . for a happier, tension-free you.

omission

The president read from the consulting company's report: "Basically, operations should be conducted according to the attached plan. . . . Several new operations personnel should . . . implement the recommended procedures."

1–39. Period Format

a. No space is placed between a decimal point and a whole number. However, within a sentence, one space follows an initial or the concluding period in an abbreviation. In typewritten copy, allow two spaces after a period at the end of a sentence.

decimal—no space

Since 1975, costs of manufacturing materials have increased *18.5* percent.

initial—one space

John *R.* Gardner was elected chairman of the committee.

abbreviation within sentence—one space

Dr. Sussman has scheduled *Mrs.* Johnson for surgery at 9 *a.m.* in Granada Hills Hospital.

end of sentence—two spaces

Please begin transcribing your notes after the morning session. I believe the gentlemen wish to have the minutes by tomorrow morning.

b. Use only one period to end a sentence, even though the sentence may end with an abbreviation.

She is scheduled to arrive between 9 and 10 a.m.

Mr. Kirk's mail is to be forwarded to his Washington, D.C., address: 1938 South Harvard Street, N.W.

c. A period is always placed inside the closing quotation mark.

Ms. Allison promptly replied, "No funding requests will be honored after July 1."

Joseph was disappointed in the magazine article "New Ideas for Home Builders."

d. A period is placed inside the closing parenthesis when the words in parentheses are a complete sentence. When words in parentheses are not a complete thought and are part of another sentence, place the period outside the closing parenthesis.

complete sentence in parentheses

Several executives left the company after the merger. (They were disappointed in the leadership of the new company.)

incomplete sentence in parentheses

Only three items were discontinued after the consulting analysts completed their investigation (last March).

Question Mark

1-40. Direct Questions

Conclude a direct question that requires an answer with a question mark.

How many times have you tried to contact Miss Wilson?

Of all the people at the board meeting, how many would you estimate were antagonistic toward the salary proposal?

1-41. Statements With Questions

a. When a sentence contains a statement followed by a direct question, conclude the sentence with a question mark. Separate the statement from the question with a comma, dash, or colon, depending upon the nature of the statement.

question mark with comma

I would recommend that we contact at least three other vendors before selecting a permanent source of supply, wouldn't you agree?

1

question mark with dash

They were satisfied with the report--weren't they?

question mark with colon

Consider the following question: how do you view the profit picture for next year?

b. A statement that is meant as a question is concluded with a question mark.

You still expect to leave for Cleveland tomorrow morning?

The conference has been delayed until April?

c. Conclude a statement that contains a short, direct question with a question mark.

It was Mr. Stevens--or was it Mrs. Harrison--who requested the stationery?

You have filed your income tax return, have you not, for the last taxable year?

d. A period, rather than a question mark, is placed after an indirect question.

Mr. Holcomb asked when we expected our Albany office to release the information.

Ms. Holdridge inquired as to the possibility of placing several students in our Accounting Department as trainees in a cooperative work-experience program.

e. Polite requests phrased as questions are followed by periods rather than question marks because they are considered to be commands. A polite request (1) asks the reader to take a specific action and (2) is answered by having the reader either take or not take the action requested.

Will you please send us three copies of your latest financial report.

May I please have this information by the end of the month.

1-42. Expressions of Doubt

Doubt in expressing statements of fact may be signified by enclosing a question mark in parentheses.

His last visit to the East Coast was in 1976(?).

She earns $900(?) a month.

1-43. Series of Questions

When a sentence contains a series of questions, place a question mark at the end of each element. Only the initial letter of the sentence is capitalized, unless the element begins with a proper noun or is a complete thought.

series of incomplete questions

What are the primary responsibilities of the president? of the executive vice-president? of the treasurer?

Who requested the report--the vice-president? the secretary? the treasurer?

series of proper noun questions

Will the new flight routes stop in San Diego? Los Angeles? San Francisco?

series of independent questions

Several important issues were discussed at the conference last week: What style trends will be popular during the next decade? What comfort demands will the public make on furniture manufacturers? How much will price influence consumer furniture purchases?

1-44. Question Mark Placement

a. Question marks may be placed either inside or outside the closing quotation mark or parenthesis. When a complete question is contained within the quotation or parenthetical remark, place the question mark inside the closing quotation mark or parenthesis. If the entire sentence, not just the quotation or parenthetical remark, comprises the question, place the question mark outside the closing quotation mark or parenthesis. Use only one concluding mark at the end of a sentence.

complete question contained in parentheses

We received official notification last week *(did your notice arrive yet?)* that we must vacate our offices by the first of the month.

The committee informed me that J. Wilson Edwards has been appointed manager of the Phoenix office. *(Did you approve this appointment?)*

complete question contained in quotation marks

"*Will the entire original cast be present for the opening night in Philadelphia?*" asked a local reporter.

question encompasses entire sentence

Can you let us know your decision by March 21 (earlier if possible)?

Have you finished reading the article "Hidden Magic"?

b. If the entire sentence and the quotation are both questions, use only the first question mark—the one appearing inside the closing quotation mark.

Did the president ask, "When will the directors hold their next meeting?"

c. Leave one space after a question mark that appears within a sentence and two spaces after a question mark that appears at the end of a sentence.

1

one space

Shall I place these supplies on the desk? in the cabinet? in the storeroom?

two spaces

What time shall we leave for the airport?   When is your flight scheduled to depart?   What time do you expect to arrive in Atlanta?

Exclamation Point

1–45. Use of Exclamation Point

To express a high degree of emotion, use an exclamation point after a word, phrase, clause, or sentence.

word

What! You mean the materials will not arrive until next week?

phrase

How beautiful! The designer certainly used a great deal of color and imagination in creating this pattern.

clause

If he comes! He'd better come, or Mr. Harrison will get a new assistant.

sentence

So, she finally answered my question!

1–46. Exclamation Point Placement

a. If the typewriter does not have an exclamation point key, form the exclamation point by typing the apostrophe, back-spacing, and then typing a period.

b. The exclamation point should be used sparingly in business correspondence, and one exclamation point directly following another should be avoided. Instead, use commas, periods, or question marks to complete an exclamatory thought.

exclamation with comma

Oh, it will be impossible for us to meet the contract deadline!

exclamation with period

No! Mr. Jones has not resigned.

exclamation with question mark

What! You expected the completed analysis last week?

1

c. Exclamation points may be placed before or after the closing quotation mark or parenthesis. When a complete exclamatory remark is a quotation or is enclosed in parentheses, place the exclamation point inside the closing quotation mark or parenthesis. If the entire sentence, not just the quotation or parenthetical element, comprises the exclamatory expression, place the exclamation point outside the closing quotation mark or parenthesis. Use only one concluding mark at the end of a sentence.

complete exclamatory expression in quotation marks

One of the employees shouted, *"Break down the door!"*

complete exclamatory expression in parentheses

He obtained the help of several advisors *(what a mistake that was!)* to assist him in selecting the project subcontractors.

Management was shocked at the employees' reactions to the new process. *(Only 4 percent of the staff agreed to follow the new procedures!)*

exclamatory expression encompasses entire sentence

If you wish to take advantage of these bargains, you will have to act now (today)!

I cannot believe Marie Huffinger's statement, "Only 3 percent of the merchandise was returned"!

Quotation Marks

1–47. Direct Quotations

Place direct quotations, the exact wording used by a writer or speaker, within quotation marks. Quotation marks are not used for indirect quotations that do not use the exact wording of the reference.

direct quotation

"The economy cannot help but slow down by next year," said Dr. Roger Watson, a renowned economist.

indirect quotation

Donna Roberts, our production manager, said that our manufacturing costs per unit will increase at least 30 percent within the next year.

1–48. Short Expressions

a. When short expressions—such as words used in humor, technical words used in a nontechnical way, or slang words—need to be emphasized or clarified for the reader, they are placed in quotation marks. These same words are often shown in italics when they appear in print.

1

slang words

My secretary was certainly "on the ball" when she discovered the error in the contract.

technical words used in nontechnical way

Mr. Rollins announced that "all systems are go" for the new space exploration project.

b. Place in quotation marks the definitions of words or expressions. Underscore the word or expression defined.

defined word

According to some economists, a recession is actually a "little depression."

defined expression

The French term faux pas means "a social blunder."

1–49. Titles

Titles of various kinds of literary or artistic works such as magazine or newspaper articles, chapters of books, movies, television shows, plays, poems, lectures, songs, and themes are placed within quotation marks. Names of books, magazines, pamphlets, and newspapers, however, are underscored or typed in all capital letters.

chapter and book title

The chapter "Principles of Office Organization" contained in Office Management and Automation was helpful in implementing our office reorganization.

movie title

Disney's "Cinderella" has been a favorite of children for many years.

lecture title

Her lecture "Combating Inflationary Trends" was very well attended.

song title

We arrived at the musical just in time to hear "With a Little Bit of Luck."

1–50. Quotations Within Quotations

Use single quotation marks to signify a quotation within a quotation. Single quotation marks are typed by using the apostrophe key.

The report stated, "According to the U.S. Chamber of Commerce, 'The problem of air and water pollution must be solved within the next decade if our cities are to survive.' "

1–51. Quoted Paragraphs

a. When a quoted paragraph contains fewer than four lines and consists of two or more sentences, place quotation marks at the beginning of the first sentence and at the end of the last sentence.

Mr. Williams wrote: "My wife became ill on Monday and was taken to the hospital. Therefore, I will not be able to attend the meeting."

b. When a quotation contains four lines or more, indent and single-space the quoted material. No quotation marks are used with the quotation. Introduce the quotation with a colon.

The speaker brought out the importance of management communication when she made the following statement:

To exercise the function of leadership, there must be effective communication. If a leader cannot communicate, there is no leader because information cannot pass between the two groups. For instance, in management, it is not possible to delegate duties and authority without effective communication.

1–52. Ellipsis

An ellipsis, a series of three periods with a space before and after each period, is used to show an intentional omission of quoted material. If the omission occurs at the end of a sentence, use an ellipsis, leave a space, and then place the closing punctuation mark for the sentence. If one or more sentences have been omitted, first place the closing punctuation mark immediately after the last word; then follow with an ellipsis to show the omission.

omission within sentence

The new sign was worded to discourage nonresidents from parking in the private lot: "Violators will be towed . . . cars will be released only upon payment of a $50 fine."

end of sentence omission

The guarantee reads: "All repairs that do not come under the warranty will be made at less than 30 percent of the regular cost . . . ."

"How many miles is the home office from our various branch offices; i.e., Houston, Dallas, Oklahoma City, . . . ?"

one or more sentences omitted

"Please ship our foreign orders by September 1. . . . Our European distributors must have their merchandise by October 1." (Double-space after final period in ellipsis before beginning the next sentence.)

"Will you be able to attend the conference in Baltimore? . . . We will need to set up our display booths on September 9." (Double-space after final period in ellipsis before beginning next sentence.)

1–53. Capitalization With Quotation Marks

a. Capitalize the first word of a complete sentence enclosed in quotation marks.

"Please call me before 10 a.m. tomorrow," requested Mrs. Edwards.

Andrew replied, "Yes, I will be able to attend the conference on Monday."

b. Capitalize incomplete thoughts enclosed in parentheses only if the quoted words themselves are capitalized. Quoted expressions preceded by "stamped" or "marked" are usually capitalized.

capitalized

His check was returned from the bank marked "Insufficient Funds."

"Handle With Care" was stamped on the package.

not capitalized

Ms. Atkins asked us to spend "as little time as possible" on this project.

1–54. Quotation Mark Placement

a. Periods and commas are always placed inside the closing quotation mark; semicolons and colons, outside the closing quotation mark.

period

The purchase requisition reads, "Cancel this order if the merchandise cannot reach us by the first of the month."

comma

"Our operating costs must be lowered," said Mr. Collins.

semicolon

The consultant's report stated, "A thorough analysis of the company's data processing system should be made"; however, no steps have been taken to initiate such an analysis.

colon

Miss Cox recommended the following vacation policy "unless a better one can be found": (1) Employees should select their vacation time on the basis of seniority and (2) conflicts should be resolved by the employees themselves, whenever possible.

b. When a complete question or exclamation is contained within the quotation, place the question mark or exclamation point inside the closing quotation mark. If the entire sentence comprises the question or exclamation, then place the appropriate mark outside the closing quotation mark. If both the quotation and the entire sentence are questions, use only the first question mark.

complete question within quotation

He asked, "Where are the annual reports filed?"

entire sentence comprises question

Do you have a copy of her latest article, "Air Pollution Control"?

complete exclamation within quotation

"Do not," exclaimed Mr. Rey, "leave the lights burning all night again!"

entire sentence comprises exclamation

Our new sales manager is a real "go-getter"!

question within a question

Did Mr. Heinze inquire, "What time will our flight depart?"

Apostrophe

1–55. Possessives

a. When a noun, singular or plural, does not end in an *s* sound, add an apostrophe and *s* (*'s*) to form the possessive case.

singular noun

Yes, I found the request on my *secretary's* desk.

plural noun

Women's fashions are much more colorful this year.

b. When a noun, singular or plural, ends in an *s* sound, generally add only an apostrophe (*'*) to form the possessive case. However, an apostrophe and *s* (*'s*) *may* be added to singular nouns ending in an *s* sound if the additional *s* sound is pronounced.

singular noun

Mrs. Simons' attendance record has been perfect during the last five years.

plural noun

Customers' accounts must be reviewed every 90 days.

singular noun with additional "s" sound

We have been invited to our *boss's* home for dinner on April 15.

c. Possessives are generally formed from nouns that represent people or animals (animate objects) or nouns relating to time, distance, value, or celestial bodies. For other types of nouns (inanimate objects), show possession by an *of* phrase.

1

animate possessive

The *employees'* picnic is scheduled for next Saturday.

time possessive

This *year's* profit and loss statement showed a gain of nearly 12 percent.

value possessive

She ordered several thousand *dollars'* worth of paper.

celestial possessive

During the summer months the *sun's* rays can be extremely harmful if one is not careful.

distance possessive

He came within a *hair's* breadth of hitting the parked car.

inanimate possessive

The *terms of the loan* were extended another six months.

d. Form the possessive of compound nouns by having the last word show possession.

She was designated her *father-in-law's* beneficiary.

Our next Christmas party will be held at the *chairman-of-the-board's* home.

e. When two or more nouns have joint possession, only the last noun shows possession. When the nouns represent individual ownership, however, each noun must show possession.

joint possession

Bill and Sheryl's new secretary had worked at ABCO Corporation for three years.

individual possession

Mary's and Henry's new secretaries had worked in the clerical pool for over a year.

f. The possessive of indefinite pronouns such as *anyone, everyone, someone, anybody, everybody, somebody,* and *nobody* is formed by using the same rules that apply to possessive nouns.

It is *anyone's* guess when we will be able to resume production.

Somebody's car is blocking the entrance to the parking lot.

g. The possessive forms of personal or relative pronouns (such as *its, theirs, whose,* or *yours*) do not include apostrophes. These pronouns are often confused with verb contractions, all of which contain apostrophes.

possessive pronoun

I met Ralph, *whose* father has a large account with our organization.

contraction

I met Sara, *who's* going to apply for a job with our firm.

possessive pronoun

Although the company had *its* greatest sales volume last year, it still failed to show a profit.

contraction

It's impossible to read his handwriting.

h. Possessives of abbreviations are formed by using the same rules that apply to possessive nouns.

noun not ending with "s"

The *CPA's* report was comprehensive.

noun ending with "s"

Barker Bros.' annual sale will be held next week.

i. Use the possessive case of a noun or pronoun before a gerund (an *-ing* verb used as a noun).

noun

Don's accounting of the convention expenses was incomplete.

pronoun

We would appreciate *your* returning the enclosed form by March 31.

j. Sometimes an explanatory expression, instead of the noun it modifies, shows possession. When this form of writing sounds awkward, show possession by using an *of* phrase.

apostrophe

It was Ms. Madden, our *office manager's,* idea to hold the meeting.

"of" phrase

It was the idea *of our office manager,* Ms. Madden, to hold the meeting.

k. Many organizations with plural possessives in their names have omitted the apostrophe; organizations with singular possessives have tended to retain the apostrophe. The precise format used by the organization itself should be followed.

1

plural possessive

We have just been granted a loan from the *Farmers* Bank and Trust Company.

singular possessive

The contract was issued to *Linton's* Manufacturing Company.

1–56. Additional Uses

a.   Use the apostrophe to form contractions.

single-word contraction

acknowledged   *ack'd*

two-word contraction

is not   *isn't*

b.   The apostrophe is used to form the plural of letters, numbers, and words used as words.

plural of letter

Mr. Craig's daughter received three *A's* on her report card.

plural of numbers

Please write your *7's* and *1's* more legibly.

plural of words used as words

Miss Orson uses too many *"you know's" in her speaking.*

Parentheses

1–57. Nonessential Expressions

Parentheses are used to set off and subordinate nonessential expressions that would otherwise confuse the reader because (1) they give supplementary information that has no direct bearing on the main idea or (2) they call for an abrupt change in thought. References and directions are examples of expressions that are often enclosed in parentheses.

abrupt change in thought

I wrote Mr. Furstman (I tried to call him, but there was no answer) and asked him to contact us before October 4.

reference

All major repairs must first be cleared through proper channels. (See Bulletin 8 dated March 2.)

1

directions

Please run off 100 copies of this stencil by tomorrow. (Center the material and use yellow paper.)

1–58. Numerals

Numerals in legal, business, and professional documents are often shown in parentheses to confirm a spelled-out figure.

All work is guaranteed for ninety (90) days.

Compensation for services rendered will not exceed three thousand dollars ($3,000).

1–59. Enumerated Items

Enclose numbers or letters in parentheses when they are used to enumerate lists of items within a sentence.

numbers

I need the following information for the current year: (1) the number of people hired, (2) the number of people laid off, and (3) the number of people terminated.

letters

Please send us the following information: (a) current salary trends, (b) unemployment statistics, and (c) placement requests.

1–60. Parentheses Placement

a. Words, phrases, and clauses enclosed in parentheses in the middle of a sentence function as part of the sentence in applying rules of punctuation and capitalization.

word

We will fly to Oakland *(California)* for our annual convention.

phrase

Ms. Haven will gross nearly $800,000 *(as compared to a $500,000 average)* in sales this year.

clause

Our new manager *(several members of our staff met him last week)* will conduct a communications seminar in the spring.

b. When a period is used to close a sentence that ends with an incomplete thought enclosed in parentheses, place the period outside the closing parenthesis.

1

According to our latest reports, this procedure violates state laws (Minnesota and Wyoming).

Several members of the committee will meet in Kansas City this weekend (if possible).

c. When a period is used to close a sentence that ends with a complete thought enclosed in parentheses, the two elements are treated separately. Place a period at the end of both thoughts, with the final period appearing inside the closing parenthesis.

Yes, your order is on its way. (I mentioned this fact to your secretary yesterday.)

Several members of our staff attended the ATLW conference this year. (It was held in Hawaii.)

d. If a word, phrase, or clause shown in parentheses requires a question mark or exclamation point, use such a mark of punctuation only if the sentence ends with a *different mark.*

parenthetical question

Our new manager (do you know Marsha Karl?) will arrive in Los Angeles tomorrow.

Were you informed that our new price list (has your copy arrived yet) will go into effect on October 1?

parenthetical exclamation

Have you heard about the enormous price increases (I can scarcely believe them!) in single-family homes?

Prices in this tourist town are high (unusually high)!

e. Place commas, semicolons, and colons outside the closing parenthesis.

comma

If you plan to attend the company party (on May 16), please send your reservations to Miss Terry Thomsen by Monday, May 12.

semicolon

His report dealt with the importance of our country's major transportation agencies (railroads, inland waterways, motor trucks, pipe lines, air transportation, express, and parcel post); therefore, little emphasis was given to rising transportation costs.

colon

On February 15 Ms. Pangonis will introduce two new product lines (in our women's fashion department): the Sportswoman Series and the Sun and Surf Coordinates.

Brackets

1–61. Use of Brackets

Brackets are generally used to insert remarks or set off editorial corrections in material written by someone else. In addition, use brackets to enclose the term *sic* (meaning *thus* or *so*) to show that an error in quoted material appeared in the original document.

In his report Mr. Gilmer stated: "With new equipment to speed up the production process [*he did not specify what new equipment was needed*], substantial savings can be mad [*sic*] in both material and labor costs."

1–62. Brackets Placement

The placement of other punctuation marks with brackets follows the same principles outlined for parentheses in 1-60.

Asterisk

1–63. Use of Asterisk

When a footnote needs to be called to the reader's attention, use an asterisk. The asterisk generally follows other punctuation marks, except when it is used with a dash or with a complete thought enclosed in parentheses.

after most punctuation marks

A government report states, "Air traffic is expected to double in the next decade."*

before parenthesis or dash

Very good results have been obtained by companies who have hired outside consultants to develop cost-cutting procedures. (Several articles have recently appeared in professional journals attesting to this fact.*)

Diagonal

1–64. Use of Diagonal

Use the diagonal line between (1) letters in some abbreviations, (2) numerals in fractions, and (3) the expression *and/or* to indicate the terms are interchangeable. No space is left before or after the diagonal.

abbreviation

Please address the envelope: Mrs. Adeline Price, *c/o* George Martin, Display

1

Manager, Wilson Disc Company, 1141 Western Avenue, Los Angeles, California 90024.

fraction

Costs have increased ½ percent since last week.

and/or

Authorizations for future purchases may be obtained from Jorgensen *and/or* Kline.

Underscore

1-65. Use of the Underscore

The underscore is used to emphasize such items as headings; words that would normally be italicized in print; and titles of books, magazines, newspapers, or complete published works. Continuous lines, with no spacing between words, are used for underscoring. Except for periods with abbreviations, punctuation marks immediately following underlined material are not underlined.

word italicized in print

He always misspells the word convenience.

magazine title

According to an article in Business Week, most movies are currently being filmed outside the United States.

abbreviation

Be sure to place a.m. in lowercase letters.

Ampersand

1-66. Use of the Ampersand

The ampersand (&), a symbol that represents the word *and*, is primarily used in the official name of some business organizations.

ampersand in company name

Johnson & Johnson was the subcontractor for the project.

use of "and" in company name

All merger talks with Merritt *and* Sons have been delayed until the end of our fiscal period.

Hyphenating Words

2–1. Compound Words

a. Often two or more words act as single thought units. Nouns and verbs in this category may be written as separate words, written as single words, or hyphenated. Consult an up-to-date dictionary to determine the exact form of compound verbs and nouns.*

separate words, nouns

sales tax	double boiler	notary public	editor in chief

single words, nouns

bookcase	checkbook	lawsuit	heavyweight

hyphenated words, nouns

light-year	brother-in-law	attorney-at-law	trade-off

single words, verbs

to uphold	to typewrite	to downgrade	to landscape

hyphenated words, verbs

to double-cross	to air-condition	to triple-space	to co-star

b. When two or more words act as a *single* adjective (compound adjective) and are placed *before* a noun, they are hyphenated. The hyphens are generally omitted when the word group appears *after* the noun.

before noun

That looks pretty good for a *last-minute* job.

The *up-to-date* filing system enabled Mr. Lopez to locate the papers immediately.

Mr. Wachs is a *house-to-house* salesperson.

after noun

That job looks pretty good for being done at the *last minute*.

These files are no longer *up to date*.

My daughter went *house to house* to collect money for the Cancer Fund.

c. Some compound adjectives are so well known that the hyphen is no longer needed to indicate a single thought unit.

---

*Based upon *Webster's New Collegiate Dictionary* (Springfield, Mass.: G. & C. Merriam Company, 1977).

51

charge account customer	word processing center
high school teacher	golf club cover
data processing equipment	blue plate luncheon
income tax return	early bird special
department store personnel	court reporting school
mobile home sales	home loan applications

d. When two proper nouns are used as a single adjective before another noun, the proper nouns are hyphenated. The elements of a single proper noun are not hyphenated, however, when they are used as an adjective.

two proper nouns used as an adjective

Yes, we have many *Mexican-American* employees.

The *Los Angeles-San Francisco* flight takes about one hour.

single proper noun used as an adjective

Mrs. Meyers had her mail forwarded to a *Wilshire Boulevard* address.

The *Pierce College* band plays at every football game.

e. Adverbs ending in *ly* that are combined with adjectives are not hyphenated.

Mr. Stevens was the most *smartly dressed* man at the meeting.

Everyone knows that George is an *amazingly perceptive* man.

f. When the first word of a compound is a comparative or a superlative ending in *er* or *est*, the compound is not hyphenated.

If he had used *heavier handed* methods, he would now be the *highest paid* person in the department.

g. When a series of hyphenated adjectives have a common ending, use suspending hyphens.

Ms. Coleman anticipates that at least a *two- or three-week* study of the problem will be necessary.

The meeting was called to develop both *long- and short-term* objectives for the company.

2-2. Prefixes

a. Word beginnings *ex* (meaning "former"), *self*, and *vice* are usually hyphenated. Words beginning with *pre*, *re*, and *non* are not hyphenated. Words beginning with *co* may or may not be hyphenated. Use your dictionary to check the hyphenation of words with these beginnings.

"ex," "self," "vice"

The *ex-baseball hero* is now in the real estate business.

She is very *self-confident* about her work.

Who will be the new executive *vice-president* of your firm?

2

"pre," "re," "non"

All our diapers are *prefolded*.

Where will the *preemployment* interviews be held?

All ropes must be *recoiled* neatly and put away at the end of the day.

Please have the tires on the truck *realigned*.

Tuition reimbursements will not be made to *nonaccredited* educational institutions.

Please initiate legal proceedings against Phillips Bros. for *nonpayment* of their account.

"co"

co-edition	coauthor
co-star	coed
co-worker	copilot

b.   When a prefix is added to a proper noun, place a hyphen between the prefix and the proper noun.

We found that many firms operating today date back to *pre-Civil War* times.

If you cannot promise a *mid-September* delivery date, cancel the order.

To some people a 4th of July without fireworks would be *un-American*.

2-3. Numbers

a.   Compound numbers from *21* to *99* are hyphenated when they appear in written form.

Ninety-six responses to the questionnaire have been returned so far, but *twenty-four* are still missing.

b.   In numbers over 100, elements other than compound numbers are not hyphenated.

The lessee shall pay a sum of *two thousand eight hundred and seventy-five* dollars ($2,875) to the lessor.

c.   When a number and a noun function as a single unit in describing another noun (compound adjective), separate the words in the compound adjective with a hyphen. Only in percentages and numbers over 100 are the hyphens omitted.

hyphen—compound adjective

We have a *three-year* lease on this building.

2

Our freeways have a *55-mile-an-hour* speed limit.

She was charged a *25-cent* toll for using the speedway.

no hyphen—percentage

We have had a *25 percent* sales increase during the past year.

no hyphen—number over 100

Ridgewood, Inc., announced a *$3 million* profit for the year.

d.   The hyphen may be used to replace the terms *to* or *through* between two numerals.

Your vacation will be July *3–18* this year.

Refer to pages *70–75* for further instructions.

Dividing Words

2–4.   When Not to Divide Words

Dividing words at the end of a line should generally be avoided because complete words are easier to understand, easier to read, and neater in appearance.

a.   Do not divide words of one syllable.

one-syllable words

bread   thought   night   through

one-syllable "ed" words

weighed   tired   banked   shipped

b.   Do not divide words containing six or fewer letters.

number   office   copier   fewer   only

c.   Do not divide words if only one or two letters in a word are to be separated.

one letter

a ward   radi o

two letters

en large   present ed

d.   Do not divide proper nouns, titles, numerals, abbreviations, or contractions.

54

proper nouns

Mississippi   Christopher   Los Angeles

titles

Professor   Governor   Lieutenant

numerals

$10,875   2,835,793   1,146

abbreviations

NASA   UNESCO   IBRAC   Ph.D.

contractions

haven't   shouldn't   can't

e. Do not divide closely related combinations such as month and day, month and year, courtesy title and surname, surname and abbreviation, or numeral and descriptive unit (except as shown by the slashes in the following examples).

month and day

December 12   June 3   April 15

month and year

June 1967   January 1979   December 1940

courtesy title and surname

Mr. DeLong   Ms. Rhodes   Dr. Ledbetter

surname and abbreviations

John T. / Stevens, Jr.   Alice / Duffy, CPA
LeMoyne / Mark, Esq.   William Bruce / Roberts, III

numeral and descriptive unit

9 a.m.   page 83   5:30 p.m.

6 ounces   Model 18   12 meters

80 percent   line 4   27 cents

f. Do not divide the last words of more than two consecutive lines.

g. Avoid dividing a word at the end of the first line of a paragraph.

h. Avoid dividing a word that concludes the last full line of a paragraph.

i. Do not divide the last word on a page.

2–5. When to Divide Words*

a. Divide words between syllables.

dex ter ous   jour ney   mis pro nounce

b. Divide hyphenated and other compound words at their natural breaks.

hyphenated compound

self-/esteem   vice-/president

one-word compound

common/place   hand/made   break/down

c. When possible, divide a word after a prefix or before a suffix. One- and two-letter prefixes and suffixes, however, are not separated from the rest of the word.

prefix

anti body   pre condition   mis fortune

suffix

evasive ness   inspira tion   oversell ing

one- and two-letter prefixes

amoral   unhappy   restate

one- and two-letter suffixes

equity   fully   brotherly   taxi

d. Words may be divided between double letters except when the root word itself ends with a double letter and is followed by a suffix such as *able, ing,* and *ness.*

double letters divided

bul letin   suc cess   oscil late

double letters not divided

distill able   merciless ness   bless ing

e. Divide words between two vowels that are pronounced separately.

extenu ating   *appreci ative*   *continu ation*

---

*When in doubt, you should consult a word division manual such as *Webster's Instant Word Guide*, published by G. & C. Merriam Company.

f. Divide words *after*, not before, a single vowel except when the vowel is part of the suffix.

after a single vowel

assimi late   bene factor   clari fication

vowel part of suffix

accept able   forc ible   favor ably

2–6. Division of Word Groups

a. Dates may be divided between the day and the year, but not between the month and the day.

Miss Johnson plans to participate from July 1,
1974, until June 30, 1977.

b. Full names of individuals may be divided between the first and last names or after the middle initial.

Within the next few weeks, Mr. Harrison E.
Petrowski will interview several job applicants.

c. Names preceded by long titles may be separated from their titles.

We sent several copies of our book to Professor
George L. Rodriguez.

d. In street addresses divide between the street name and the words *Street, Avenue, Boulevard,* etc. If the street name contains more than one word, the address may also be broken after the first word.

We are sending your order to 18932 Glenview
Drive, Reston, Virginia 22091.

Our new offices are located at 849 West 73
Street in downtown Philadelphia.

e. In addresses, divide geographical locations only between the city and state, not between the state and zip code.

Please send it to 1183 Noble Drive, Sepulveda,
California 91343.

f. A numbered or lettered list may be broken directly before the letter or number, but not directly after.

The affirmative action officer gave these reasons: (1) fewer job openings in the teaching profession, (2) enrollment declines in the student population, and (3) increase in the mandatory retirement age for teachers.

g. A sentence with a dash may be broken after the dash, but not directly before it.

Your new policy on recruitment is excellent—
a step in the right direction.

At the end of the year—possibly in December—
we are planning to take a trip to the Orient.

2

3
CAPITALIZATION

Capitalization Solution Finder

Capitalization Solution Finder (continued)

3

General Format

3–1. **Beginning Words**

a. Capitalize the beginning words of sentences, quoted sentences, independent phrases, lines of poetry, and items in an outline.

sentence

All employees are requested to work overtime until the inventory has been completed.

quoted sentence

The guarantee states, "*Defective* parts will be replaced free of charge."

independent phrase

Now, to the important point.

poetry

By the rude bridge that arched the flood,
Their flag to the April's breeze unfurled,
Here once the embattled farmers stood,
And fired the shot heard round the world.
—Emerson

outline

1. *Specific* instructions
    a. *Type* of correspondence
    b. *Number* of carbon copies
    c. *Special* mailing notations

b. The initial letter of an incomplete quoted thought is not capitalized unless the first word (1) is a proper noun, (2) is capitalized for another rule of capitalization, or (3) is preceded by identification words such as *marked* or *stamped*.

lowercase

Mr. Reyes was directed to "take care of this situation immediately."

proper noun

Mr. Stone's curt answer was "George will take care of it."

rule of capitalization

My favorite song in the production is "My Boy Bill."

preceded by identification words "marked" or "stamped"

This package should be stamped "First Class Mail."

Your check was returned by the bank marked "Insufficient Funds."

c. In correspondence the beginning words of the salutation and complimentary close are capitalized. Any nouns included in the salutation should be capitalized, but any intervening adjectives should not.

salutations

Dear Mr. Jones   *Gentlemen*   *My* dear *Friend*

complimentary closes

Sincerely yours   *Cordially* yours   *Yours* very truly

d. When the words preceding a colon introduce a complete thought that presents a rule or requires emphasis, capitalize the first word after the colon. Also, if the material following a colon consists of two or more sentences or begins an enumeration on the following line, capitalize the beginning word. Always capitalize proper nouns. In other cases, do not capitalize the first word following a colon.

rule following colon

Please apply the following in typing our office correspondence: *Use* modified block format with mixed punctuation.

item of special emphasis following colon

Note: *Several* of our employees were listening to the World Series during working hours.

two or more sentences following colon

Here are two important points to consider: *In* the first place, will it be economically feasible for us to enlarge our facilities at this time? Second, is the current market able to assimilate the increased production?

enumeration beginning on following line

Please send us copies of the following items:

1. *Lease* agreement with Property Management Associates
2. *Statement* of rental income for 1979
3. *List* of expenses for 1980

proper noun

Three colleges are involved in the project: *DeKalb* Community College, MiraCosta College, and the City College of New York.

first word not capitalized

We need to order the following garden supplies: *lawn* seed, liquid fertilizer, and insect spray.

Our production schedule is experiencing a two months' delay: *the* warehouse fire set us back considerably.

e. The first word of a complete thought contained in parentheses is not capitalized if it appears within a sentence unless the word is a proper noun. A complete thought contained in parentheses that appears immediately after a sentence is treated as a separate unit, and the first word is capitalized.

lowercase within sentence

Several minor changes (*these* were recommended by Mr. Lloyd) will be made in the final draft.

proper noun capitalized within sentence

Your recommendations (Ms. Williams approved all of them) will be incorporated into the marketing survey.

capitalized at end of sentence

A group of marketing students wish to tour our main plant in Atlanta, Georgia. (*The* students will arrange for their own transportation.)

3–2. Proper Nouns and Adjectives

a. Proper nouns (words that name a particular person, place, or thing) and adjectives derived from proper nouns are capitalized. Capitalize the names of persons, places, geographic localities, streets, parks, buildings, shopping centers, developments, ships, airplanes, etc.

proper nouns

We have opened a new branch office in *Austin, Texas.*

I will meet you at the top of the *Empire State Building.*

The *Orange County Fair* will be held in *Petit Park* this year.

When will the *Brownsville Shopping Mall* be ready for occupancy?

We flew to Florida on a *Boeing 747* to meet our cruise ship, the *Song of Norway.*

adjectives derived from proper nouns

She ordered eight place settings of *Franciscan* china.

The *Socratic* method is often used in debates.

b. When well-known descriptive terms such as nicknames are used in place of proper nouns, they are capitalized.

My territory includes sales districts west of the *Rockies*. (Rocky Mountains)

Most of his business trips have been to the *Windy City*. (Chicago)

Old Hickory was particularly popular with the frontiersmen. (Andrew Jackson)

c. Sometimes proper nouns, such as widely used commercial products, acquire common noun meanings through popular usage. As a result, they are not capitalized. Always capitalize, however, specific trade names of products. The product itself is not capitalized unless it is a coined derivation that is considered part of the trade name.

common noun meanings

Please run 20 *mimeograph* copies of this memo.

Yes, *india* ink was included in the order.

We are out of stock on that particular brand of *french* dressing.

trade names with common-noun products

Did you order a *Sony* portable television set?

Our new *Frigidaire freezer* was delivered today.

Please deliver the *Kirby vacuum* to Dr. Iannizzi's home.

trade names and products capitalized

Your *Amana Radarange* will give you many years of service.

Next week we will install a *Griffin Mail-O-Meter* in our office.

3–3. Abbreviations

Most abbreviations are capitalized only if the words they represent are capitalized.

lowercase

Please send 5 *doz.* hammers *c.o.d.*

You may contact me any time after 5:30 *p.m.*

uppercase

She sat for the *CPS* examination last May.

Mrs. Johnson was awarded a bachelor of arts degree from *UCLA* in 1977.

3–4. Numbered or Lettered Items

Nouns followed by numerals or letters are usually capitalized, except in the case of page, paragraph, line, and verse references. The word *number* is abbreviated, except when it appears at the beginning of a sentence.

uppercase

A reservation was held for you on *Flight 487* to Chattanooga.

Please check *Invoice B3721* to verify that all items have been shipped.

I believe my policy, *No. 68341*, covers the injury.

Did you receive our order for your *Model 23D* china case?

lowercase

Refer to *page 3, paragraph 2,* of the contract for the schedule of project completion.

number *at beginning of sentence*

Number 145-MD has been out of stock for over three months.

3

Titles

3–5. People

a. Capitalize the title of a person's profession, political office, rank, or family relationship when it precedes his name.

profession

The meeting will be conducted by *Professor* Sharon Jones.

political office

We are looking forward to meeting *Mayor* Barton Siller next Friday.

rank

All medical problems should be brought to the attention of *Major* Richard Cortez.

family relationship

When *Aunt* Olive arrives, we can be seated for dinner.

b. When a title follows a person's name, it is not capitalized, except in cases pertaining to high-ranking government officials (President of the United States, Vice-President of the United States, Cabinet members, governors, and Congressional senators).

regular title

Carla Irwin, *comptroller* of A & I Enterprises, wrote the report.

title of high-ranking official

George Dillon, the *Senator* from Georgia, received an award for outstanding service.

c. A person's title is not capitalized when it is followed by an appositive.

I went to see the *vice-president*, Don Curry.

She consulted with her *doctor*, Janice Montgomery, about the accident.

d. When a person's title is used in place of his name, it is generally not capitalized. However, in the case of direct address and in reference to high-ranking government officials (President of the United States, Vice-President of the United States, Cabinet members, Congressional senators, and governors), capitalize the title if it replaces the name. Do not, however, capitalize common nouns such as *sir, ladies,* or *gentlemen* used in direct address.

regular title

The *auditor* indicated our books were in order.

direct address

Did I pass the test, *Professor*?

Yes, *ladies* and *gentlemen*, I believe all our sales personnel will meet their quotas this year.

title of high-ranking official

It was a pleasure to meet the *Secretary of State* last week.

Please invite the *Governor* to attend the conference.

e. A person's title is always capitalized in business correspondence when it appears in the inside address, signature line, or envelope address.

Miss Ellen Davis, *President*

Mrs. Delieu Walters, *Personnel Director*

f. When the title of an officer is used in that organization's minutes, by-laws, or rules, it is capitalized.

The *Treasurer's* report was read and approved.

The *President* will be responsible for the negotiation of all labor contracts.

g. Descriptive terms such as *ex, elect, late,* and *former* are not capitalized when they are combined with a title.

"ex"

Since *ex*-President D. J. Morgan was appointed chairman of the board, our company has prospered.

"elect"

Councilman-*elect* Norman Rittgers will be sworn in on January 2.

"late"

The *late* President Eisenhower was an avid golfer.

"former"

A copy of the report was sent to *former* President Ford.

3–6. Literary or Artistic Works

a. Capitalize the principal words in titles of publications and other literary or artistic works such as movies, plays, songs, poems, and lectures. Articles (*a, an, the*), conjunctions (*and, but, or, nor*), and prepositions with fewer than four letters (*of, in, on, to, up,* etc.) are not capitalized unless they appear at the beginning or end of the title.

The titles of books, magazines, pamphlets, and newspapers are underscored or typed in all capital letters. Titles of other literary or artistic works are placed in quotation marks.

books

I learned a great deal from the book The Art of Readable Writing.

DuPont, the Autobiography of an American Enterprise will be available in June.

The best-seller Up Into the Wild Blue Yonder has sold over one million copies.

magazine

We have ordered the Journal of Abnormal and Social Psychology for our reference library.

play

Mr. Conway's new production, "A Comet Is Coming," will open on Broadway next week.

movie

"Snow White and the Seven Dwarfs" is scheduled for screening in neighborhood theaters next month.

b. Capitalize the main words and place in quotation marks the titles of subsections contained in books, magazines, pamphlets, or newspapers. Also capitalize the main words and place in quotation marks the titles of typewritten reports.

chapter of book

Please review carefully "Supervision of Office Personnel" in the book Office Organization and Management.

magazine article

Did you read "Word Processing Shortcuts" in the latest issue of The Executive Secretary's Journal?

newspaper column

"Jim Elwood Reports" in yesterday's Vista Daily Journal covered extensively the city council's feud with the mayor.

typewritten report

Here is your copy of "Research Personnel Available."

3–7. Academic Subjects, Courses, and Degrees

a. Titles of specific courses are capitalized but the names of academic subject areas are not, unless the subject area name contains a proper noun.

specific courses

How many students are enrolled in *Digital Computer Programming 43*?

Last year she took *Speech 125*.

subject areas

It is important that Ms. Harris take an *accounting* class this spring.

Our college offers over 20 different *history* classes.

subject area containing proper noun

I earned an "A" in my *business English* class.

b. References to academic degrees are generally not capitalized, unless they are used after the name of an individual.

general reference

Mr. Sorenson will be awarded a *bachelor of science* degree this June.

after person's name

Wilma P. Koskey, *Doctor of Divinity*, will deliver the opening address.

c. Capitalize abbreviations of academic degrees appearing after a person's name.

Dan Shriver, *D.D.S.*, is an excellent dental surgeon.

We have asked Marilyn Watson, *D.B.A.*, to be our speaker.

Make your check payable to Elbert Gann, *M.D.*

Groups, Places, Dates

3–8. Organizations

a. Principal words in the names of all organizations—business, civic, educational, governmental, labor, military, philanthropic, political, professional, religious, and social—are capitalized.

Boston Chamber of Commerce	Illinois Bar Association
Los Angeles Board of Education	Young Republican Club
Department of Motor Vehicles	National Council of Churches
Tactical Air Command	Porter Valley Country Club
United Way	Screen Actors' Guild

b. When the common noun element of an organization's name is used in place of the full name, it is generally not capitalized. In formal documents and in specific references to national government bodies, however, capitalize the shortened form.

general communication

All employees of the *company* are allowed ten days' sick leave per year.

The *board of education* met at its regular meeting yesterday to consider the school crisis.

formal communication

As agent for the *Association*, I am authorized to sign the convention contracts.

national government body

The bill is now before the *House*. (House of Representatives)

c. The title of a division or department within a business organization is usually capitalized when one employed by that organization refers to it. When reference is made to a division or department within another organization, however, the name is usually not capitalized, unless it is known definitely that the name used is the official name. Always capitalize the division or department title in a return address, an inside address, a signature block, or an envelope address.

department in own organization

Please notify the *Personnel Department* when you are going to be absent from work.

This contract must be signed by two members of the *Board of Directors*.

department in another organization—official title unknown

The efficiency of your *accounting department* can be increased by using our computer system.

department in another organization—official title known

We will send a copy of our official findings to your *Department of Research and Development.*

return address, inside address, signature block, or envelope address

Mr. George Juett, Manager, *Credit Department*

d. When the word *the* precedes a company name and is officially part of the name, it must be capitalized.

We received two letters from *The* Prudential Insurance Company.

e. Governmental terms such as *federal, government, nation,* and *constitution* are often used in place of their respective full names. Because they are used so often and are considered terms of general classification, they are not capitalized.

"federal"

Veterans Day is a holiday for all *federal* employees.

"government"

The *government* is concerned about inflation and its effect on the economy.

"nation"

The *nation* has been able to overcome a number of crises.

"constitution"

Interpretation of the *constitution* is the Supreme Court's responsibility.

3-9. Geographical Locations

a. The names of specific places such as states, cities, streets, mountains, valleys, parks, oceans, lakes, rivers, and harbors are capitalized. When geographical terms appear before the names of specific places or are used in plural form, they are not capitalized.

specific places

They live in *New York City*.

The magazine article outlined camping facilities on the *Colorado River*.

We visited *Yellowstone National Park* last June.

geographical term before specific place

They vacationed in the *state* of Utah last summer.

Will your tour include the *city* of London?

geographical term in plural form

The excursion will include trips on both the Mississippi and Missouri *rivers*.

Most of our discoveries have been in the San Bernardino and San Gorgonio *mountains*.

b. Points of the compass are capitalized when they are used as simple or compound nouns to designate *specific regions*. Points of the compass are not capitalized, however, when they are used to indicate *direction* or *general localities*.

specific regions

Firms connected with the aerospace industry are heavily concentrated in the *West* and *Southwest*.

Our company has increased its trade in the *Far East*.

The festival was held in *East Los Angeles*.

The sales of our *Southern Region* have increased 25 percent during the past year.

direction

The study recommended that our new plant be located just *north* of Baltimore.

Will the sale of our product be affected by the fact that birds fly *south* every winter?

My territory includes all states *west* of the Mississippi River.

By taking the *eastbound* on-ramp, you will get to the center of Madison.

general localities

The *southern* part of our state is suffering a severe drought.

Our customers from the *western* section of the city registered more complaints than any other sector.

Our delivery service is restricted to the *east* side of Miami.

Did you survey most of the *western* states?

c. Words derived from simple or compound nouns representing *specific regions* are capitalized.

I have often been accused of being a typical *Midwesterner*.

Southern Californians are known for their casual lifestyle.

3–10. Dates and Events

Capitalize days of the week, months of the year, holidays (including religious days), specific special events, and historical events. The names of seasons, decades, and centuries are generally not capitalized.

month

Our five-year plan should be completed by *January* 1.

holiday and day of week

Does *Christmas* fall on *Wednesday* this year?

specific special event

Our company will celebrate its *Silver Anniversary* next year.

historical event and century

The *Apollo 10* mission, which successfully put the first man on the moon, was the most dramatic event of the *twentieth century*.

season

Our greatest sale item during the *spring* is the Model 550 patio table.

decade

A number of movies involving life in the *sixties* have been released during the last year.

3–11. Ethnic References

Ethnic-related terms (references to a particular culture, language, or race) are capitalized.

language

A knowledge of both *Spanish* and *English* is required for the job.

race

The census indicated that many *Orientals* are living in this area.

culture

Cinco de Mayo is observed with many festivities in the *Mexican-American* community.

3–12. Celestial Bodies

The names of celestial bodies are generally capitalized except for the terms *earth, sun,* and *moon.* When these terms are used in conjunction with other celestial bodies, however, they are capitalized.

lowercase

Television broadcasts of the *moon* landing were viewed by millions of Americans.

uppercase

We have been studying the orbital paths of *Mars* and *Earth*.

4
numbers

Numbers Solution Finder

4

General Format

4–1. General Rules for Numbers

a. Numbers *one* through *ten* are written in words. Write numbers above *ten* in figures.

number ten or below

Only *seven* people attended the meeting.

number above ten

We received *182* complimentary letters this month.

4

b. A number that begins a sentence is expressed in word form. When the number cannot be written in one or two words, however, change the word order of the sentence so that the number does not begin the sentence.

number written in words

Twenty-four people responded to our advertisement for a stenographer.

sentence order rearranged

The questionnaire was answered by *260* respondents. (Not: *Two hundred sixty* [or *260*] respondents answered the questionnaire.)

c. Round numbers expressed as approximations may be written in words or figures. Approximations written in figures are more emphatic.

approximation written in words

Nearly *three hundred* people sent telegrams to the mayor.

approximation written in figures

He expected over *50* people for the conference.

d. Round numbers in the millions or billions may be expressed in a combination of figures and words.

round number

Captain Corbett has flown *2 million* miles since he earned his wings.

round number with fraction

Our company manufactured *3½ billion* pens last year.

round number with decimal

Will we exceed our production quota of *1.2 million?*

4–2. Related Numbers

a. Numbers used similarly in the same reference are considered related numbers and must be expressed in the same form. Therefore, write numbers *one* through *ten* in figures when they are used with related numbers above *ten*.

Of the *130* items inspected, only *2* were found to be defective.

Please send us *3* reams of bond paper, *24* shorthand notebooks, and *8* packages of carbon paper.

b. Round numbers in the millions or billions are expressed in figures when they are used with related numbers below a million or with related numbers that cannot be expressed in a combination of words and figures.

combined with number below 1 million

Our production of umbrellas rose from *970,000* to *2,000,000* this year.

combined with number over 1 million written in figures

During the past two years, our circulation has risen from nearly *3,000,000* copies to *3,875,500* copies.

c. Unrelated numbers used in the same sentence are considered individually to determine whether they should be expressed in words or figures.

unrelated numbers

Please send the *four* vice-presidents *15* copies of our monthly report.

combination of related and unrelated numbers

Our warehouse inventory of *22* dishwashers, *17* refrigerators, and *8* washing machines must be distributed among our *three* stores.

4–3. Numeral Format

a. Numerals of more than three digits are pointed off by commas. Years, house numbers, telephone numbers, zip codes, serial numbers, page numbers, and decimal fractions do not have commas. Metric measurements of five or more figures are separated into groups of three by the use of a space.

commas

9,823   128,492   2,865,395

no commas

1979   Serial No. 14896-AN   1111 Figueroa Street   page 1032

(205) 987-6132   .7534   Evansville, IN 47701

space

Our dairy delivers weekly over 45 000 liters of milk to homes in this city.

b. Two independent figures that appear consecutively (one after the other) in a sentence are separated by a comma.

At the end of *1979, 52* of the homes were still in escrow.

c. When two numbers appear consecutively and they both modify a following noun, use figure form for one number and word form for the other. Use word form for the smaller or less complex of the two numbers.

Please purchase *100 fifteen-cent* stamps from the post office.

The contractor plans to build *36 five-bedroom* houses on this land.

Ask the bank for an additional *fifty $1* bills.

d. Separate volume numbers and page references by commas. Weights, capacities, and measures that consist of several words are treated as single units and are not separated by commas.

volume and page number

This information can be found in *Volume IV, page 289.*

measure as a single unit

Mr. Knight verified that the room length measured *28 feet 4 inches.*

capacity as a single unit

In conventional terms the capacity of the pitcher is *2 quarts 1 cup.*

e. The plural of a numeral is formed by adding '*s.*

How many *7's* do you see in this serial number?

The *1900's* will be noted for man's first successes in space travel.

Figure Form

4–4. Money

a. Amounts of money $1 or over are expressed in figures. Omit the decimal and zeros in expressing whole dollar amounts, whether or not they appear with mixed dollar amounts.

money expressed in figures

We paid *$484.95* for this new typewriter.

omission of decimal and zeros

The list of purchases included items for $6.50, *$3,* $79.45, *$200,* and *$265.*

b. Amounts of money under $1 are expressed in figures combined with the word *cents* unless they are used in conjunction with amounts of $1 or over.

used with "cents"

Last week the basic bus fare was increased from *30 cents* to *35 cents*.

used with dollar sign

To mail the three reports, I paid *$.85,* $1.40, and $2 in postage.

c. Round amounts of money in millions or billions of dollars are expressed in combined word and figure form except when they are used with related dollar figures below a million or related amounts that can be expressed in figures only.

4

round amount

The cost of the new building was over *$12½ million.*

related to amount less than 1 million

We estimate that *$850,000* will be needed to equip the Wilmington plant and *$2,000,000* will be needed for the Van Nuys plant.

related to amount that can be expressed in figures only

Our sales decreased from *$12,450,000* last year to less than *$12,000,000* this year.

d. Amounts of money in legal documents are often expressed in words, followed by figures contained in parentheses.

The company shall pay up to *one thousand dollars ($1,000)* within 90 days upon receipt of a valid release statement.

4–5. Percentages and Decimals

a. Write percentages in figures followed by the word *percent*. The percent symbol (%) is used only for statistical or technical tables or forms.

"percent" used in sentence format

Our travel expenses are up *8 percent* over last year's.

This year a *12½ percent* pay increase was granted to all employees.

% used in statistical tables or forms

32.5%   80%   6%   99.9%   4.3%

b. Numbers containing decimals are expressed in figures. To prevent misreading, place a zero before a decimal that does not contain a whole number or does not begin with a zero.

decimal with whole number

Our trucks average *12.843* miles per gallon of gasoline.

decimal beginning with 0

The part had to be made within *.002* inch of specifications.

decimal without whole number or not beginning with 0

Only *0.4* percent of all the items manufactured this year were rejected because of defective workmanship.

4–6. Standard Weights and Measures

For quick comprehension, express in figures the amount something weighs or measures. Units of weight and measure (inches, feet, yards, ounces, pounds, tons, pints, quarts, gallons, each, dozens, gross, reams, degrees, etc.), however, are written out fully in words. Abbreviations or symbols representing these units are limited to use in business forms or statistical materials.

4

general use

His luggage was *3 pounds 6 ounces* overweight.

Over *2 tons* of waste material leave the plant daily.

Place the *80 reams* of duplicator paper in the storeroom.

Approximately *150 square yards* of carpeting will be needed for this office.

use for forms and statistical materials

| *4 doz.* | *12 yds.* | *84°* | *9 #* | *9 ft.* | *85 lb.* | *12 ea.* |

4–7. Metric Weights and Measures

a. The basic metric measurements consist of meters, grams, and liters. Prefixes indicating fractions and multiples of these quantities follow:

fractions

deci (1/10)   centi (1/100)   milli (1/1000)

multiples

deka ($\times$ 10)   hecto ($\times$ 100)   kilo ($\times$ 1000)

b. Express metric measurements in figures. Use a space to separate figures of five or more digits into groups of three. No space or comma is used with four-digit figures.

regular metric measures

We will be using *1.75-liter* bottles for our large-size apple juice.

Our new package of pie crust sticks weighs 11 ounces, which is equal to *311 grams* or *3.11 hectograms*.

four-digit figures

The distance to Boston is over *2000 kilometers.*

Our bakery chain ordered *1500 kilograms* of flour and *1200 kilograms* of sugar to be delivered to our bakeries throughout the country.

five-digit figures

His 5 acres is equal to approximately 2 hectares, that is, approximately *20 000 square meters.*

4

c. For general correspondence spell out units of measure. Abbreviate units of measure only in technical writing or on business forms.

general correspondence

10 millimeters   4 liters   80 kilometers

technical writing

60 mm   6 mg   25 km

4–8. Numbers Used With Words, Abbreviations, and Symbols

a. Numbers used directly with words are placed in figures. Page numbers, model numbers, policy numbers, and serial numbers are just a few of the instances in which numerals are used with words. The words preceding the numerals are usually capitalized except for *page, paragraph, line,* and *verse* references (see 3–4).

page number

You will find a picture of this economy unit on *page 21* of our current catalog.

model number

We ordered *Model 3* for our Word Processing Center.

policy and serial numbers

Please return your copy of *Policy 1284691D* to the home office.

The new *IBM Correcting Selectric typewriter, Serial No. 74603552,* was reported missing from the office.

b. Numbers used directly with abbreviations are placed in figures. Direct reference to the word *number* is the most common instance in which numerals are used with an abbreviation. The word *number* is abbreviated in this case, except when it appears at the beginning of a sentence.

We expect to replace this office furniture with your *No. 378* series.

The following checks were returned by your bank: *Nos. 487, 492, and 495.*

Numbers 381, 1209, and 1628 were the winning raffle tickets.

c. The use of symbols is generally avoided in business writing. However, for preparing invoices, charts, tables, and other business documents where space is limited, symbols are used liberally. Numbers expressed with symbols are written in figures.

2/10, N/30   8%   #455

Time

4–9. Dates

4

a. When dates are written after the month, use cardinal figures (1, 2, 3, etc.). Ordinal figures (1st, 2d, 3d, etc.) are used for expressing dates before the month or for expressing dates that stand alone.

cardinal figure

March 23, 1982, is the deadline for filing your claim.

ordinal figure

We expect payment in full by the *10th of April.*

Your reservations for the *9th* and the *24th* have been confirmed.

b. Dates used in most business correspondence are expressed in terms of month, date, and year. Dates used in military and foreign correspondence are generally expressed date, month, and year.

business correspondence

November 27, 1980

military or foreign correspondence

27 November 1980

4–10. Clock Time

a. Figures are used with either *a.m.* or *p.m.* to express the time of day. Omit the colon and zeros with even times. Either word or figure form, however, may be used with *o'clock.*

a.m.

Our next tour of the plant will begin at *9 a.m.*

p.m.

His plane was scheduled to arrive at *1 p.m.,* but the actual arrival time was *1:27 p.m.*

o'clock

We must leave here by *eight o'clock* (or *8 o'clock*) if we are to arrive at the meeting on time.

b.   Phrases such as "in the morning," "in the afternoon," or "at night" may be used with *o'clock* but not with *a.m.* or *p.m.*

Coffee breaks are scheduled at *ten o'clock in the morning* and at *three o'clock in the afternoon.*

c.   When exact hours of the day are expressed without *a.m., p.m.,* or *o'clock,* use word form. Either word or figure form may be used, however, when both hours and minutes are expressed.

hour

The party will begin at *eight* tonight.

hour and minutes

The meeting was not adjourned until *6:30* (or *six-thirty*).

The power went off at *9:05* (or *five after nine*) this morning.

d.   The terms *noon* and *midnight* may be used with or without the figure *12.*

noon

She left promptly at *noon* (or *12 noon*).

midnight

The new shift starts at *midnight* (or *12 midnight*).

4–11. Periods of Time

Periods of time are generally expressed in word form. However, when special emphasis is needed for time-period data relating to loan length, discount rates, interest rates, payment terms, credit terms, or other information dealing with business contracts, use figures.

general use

During the last *sixteen months,* we have shown a slight profit.

We have been in this location for *thirty-two years.*

business terms

This loan must be paid in full within *90 days.*

We give a 2 percent discount on all invoices paid within *10 days* upon receipt.

You have been granted a *9 percent* loan for *6 months.*

4–12. Ages and Anniversaries

Ages and anniversaries are generally written in word form. However, figures are used when an age appears directly after a person's name or when ages are expressed in terms of years, months, and sometimes days.

general expression of age

David will be *twenty-three* on August 9; his son John will be *three* on the same day.

The staff brought a cake as a surprise for Miss Chu's *fifty-first* birthday.

Employees no longer must retire at the age of *sixty-five.*

anniversary

We plan to give a party for Tod upon his *twenty-fifth* anniversary with the company.

age after name

Ms. Morgan, *47,* was promoted to office manager last week.

age in years, months, and days

According to our records, the insured was *35 years 7 months and 28 days* of age upon cancellation of the policy.

Addresses and Telephone Numbers

4–13. Addresses

a. House numbers are expressed in figures except for the house number *One.* No commas are used to separate digits in house numbers.

One Alpha Street

18817 Clearview Avenue

b. Street names that are numbered *ten* or below are expressed in words. Street names numbered above *ten* are written in figures and expressed in cardinal form when separated from the house number by a compass direction. Use the ordinal form *(st, d, th)* when the street name directly follows the house number.

street name ten or below

All visitors to New York City must stroll down *Fifth Avenue.*

street name above ten—cardinal form

His new address was listed as 3624 West *59* Place.

street name above ten—ordinal form

Will you send this order to 1111 *23d* Street.

c. Apartment numbers, suite numbers, box numbers, and rural route numbers are expressed in figure form.

1883 Creek Avenue, Apt. 4

Plaza Medical Building, Suite 102

Post Office Box 1584

Rural Route 2

4

d. Zip codes are expressed in figures (without commas) and typed a single space after the state.

sentence format

Ms. Dougherty requested that the refund be sent to her at Pasadena City College, 1570 East Colorado Boulevard, Pasadena, California *91106.*

inside address or envelope address

Mr. Arthur M. Manuel   Miss Vauncille Jones
5565½ Eighth Avenue   1073 83d Street, Apt. 2
Inglewood, CA *90305*   Glendale, CA *91202*

4–14. Telephone Numbers

Telephone numbers are expressed in figures. When used, place the area code in parentheses before the number.

telephone number

You may reach our representative at *728-1694.*

area code

Please telephone me collect at *(714) 328-5235.*

extension

We were requested to call *(213) 347-0551, Ext. 244,* within an hour.

Special Forms

4–15. Fractions

a. Express fractions in word form except when they are (1) long and awkward,

(2) combined with whole numbers, or (3) used for technical purposes. When written in words, the two parts of a fraction are separated by a hyphen.

fraction used alone

We have already met *three-fourths* of our production quota for this year.

long and awkward fraction

The study indicated that *21/200* of a second was needed for people to begin reacting in emergency situations.

fraction combined with whole number

Our new plant is *3½* miles from here.

fraction for technical use

The Supply Department is temporarily out of *⅝-inch* round-head metal screws.

b. Fractions written in figures and not found on the typewriter keyboard are formed by using the diagonal to separate the two parts. When fractions located on the keyboard are used with those not found on the keyboard, type all fractions by using the diagonal construction.

fraction not on keyboard

We shipped *7 2/3 tons of beef last week.*

combination of fractions located and not located on the keyboard

Our employees averaged *31 1/2* hours sick leave last year as compared to *24 3/4* hours this year.

4–16. Ordinals

Ordinal numbers *(first, second, third,* etc.*)* are generally expressed in word form except (1) in dates appearing before the month or standing alone and (2) in numbered street names above *ten*.

general use

Mr. Cox was elected to represent the *Thirty-fourth* Congressional District.

Mrs. Lang was criticized for managing the company according to *nineteenth* century policies.

date

Our next audit is scheduled for the *1st of August.*

Your order will be shipped by the *15th* of this month.

street

I plan to meet Mr. Joyce at noon on the corner of Main and *42d* Streets.

4–17. Roman Numerals

a.   When typing roman numerals for chapter or outline divisions, use capital letters to form the numbers. Also use capital letters for expressing years written in roman numerals.

Arabic Numeral	Roman Numeral	Arabic Numeral	Roman Numeral
1	I	16	XVI
2	II	17	XVII
3	III	18	XVIII
4	IV	19	XIX
5	V	20	XX
6	VI	30	XXX
7	VII	40	XL
8	VIII	50	L
9	IX	60	LX
10	X	70	LXX
11	XI	80	LXXX
12	XII	90	XC
13	XIII	100	C
14	XIV	1,000	M
15	XV		

b.   The preliminary sections of a report such as the letter of transmittal, the table of contents, and the list of tables are numbered with lowercase roman numerals. Number the pages consecutively using *i, ii, iii, iv, v,* etc.

5
abbreviations and contractions

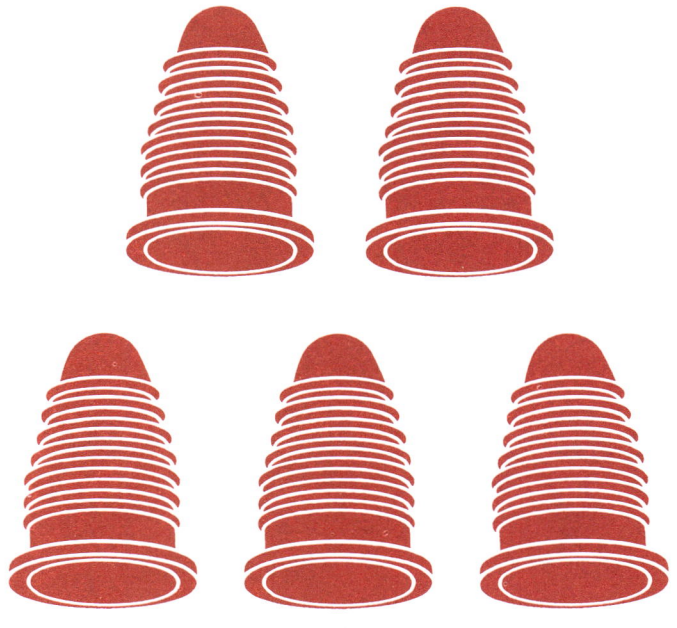

Abbreviations and Contractions Solution Finder

Abbreviations

5–1. Titles

a. The abbreviations *Mr., Ms., Mrs.,* and *Dr.* are used for courtesy titles.

Mr. Allen Davis

Ms. Phyllis Derry

Mrs. Goldstein

Dr. Lawrence Erickson

b. When civil, educational, military, and religious titles are used with the last name only, they are written out. These titles *may be* abbreviated, however, when they appear before a person's full name and brevity is required.

written out—last name only

Dear *Governor* Reece

written out—full name

I believe *Professor* Amelia Leslie is in charge of the project.

abbreviated—full name

Please invite *Lt. Col.* Donald Curry to the meeting.

c. When *Jr., Sr., Esq.,* or references to academic degrees or professional designations such as *M.D., Ph.D.,* or *CPA* are used following a person's name, they are abbreviated and capitalized. Abbreviations of academic degrees or professional designations are separated by periods, except for the designations *CPA* (Certified Public Accountant), *CPS* (Certified Professional Secretary), and *PLS* (Professional Legal Secretary).

personal title

Please send a copy of the report to Robert Lucio, *Jr.*

professional designation

Cynthia Armstrong, *CPA,* was present at the meeting.

academic title

Our new president, Armen Sarafian, *Ph.D.,* met with the Board of Directors yesterday.

5–2. Organizations

a. The names of well-known business, educational, governmental, military, labor, philanthropic, professional, and other organizations or agencies may be abbreviated. No periods are used to separate the individual letters.

A & P	AMA	FCC	NBC	SAC
AAA	CBS	NAACP	NCR	TWA
AFL-CIO	FBI	NASA	NYU	UN

b. In the names of business firms, *Co., Corp., Inc., Ltd., Mfg.,* or other parts of the firm name are abbreviated only if they are abbreviated in the official name of the organization.

We ordered the parts from Corway *Mfg. Co.*

Johnson Products, *Inc.,* will receive the contract.

5–3. Dates and Time

a. Spell out the days of the week and the months of the year. They may be abbreviated, however, when space is limited, for example, in a list of dates in a table or other illustration.

The next meeting will be held on *Monday, January 18.*

Next *Tuesday, October 8,* will mark our fifth anniversary.

b. The abbreviations *a.m. (ante meridiem)* and *p.m. (post meridiem)* are used for expressing clock time. They are typed in lowercase letters separated by periods.

Would you prefer to take the flight at *8:45 a.m.* or the one at *2 p.m.?*

He arrived at *3:30 p.m.*

c. The time zones, *EST* (Eastern Standard Time), *CST* (Central Standard Time), *MST* (Mountain Standard Time), and *PST* (Pacific Standard Time), are abbreviated. When daylight saving time is in effect, the time zones are referred to as *EDT, CDT, MDT,* and *PDT.*

According to the latest schedule, his plane will arrive in Denver at 6 p.m., *MST.*

The new schedules were based on *EDT.*

d. The abbreviations *B.C.* (before Christ) and *A.D. (anno Domini)* are sometimes used in expressing dates. Both follow the year and are typed in capital letters with periods. In formal writing, however, *A.D.* may appear before the year.

B.C.

He claims that the statue dates back to *400 B.C.*

A.D. after the year

Her thesis dealt with the rise of Christianity from *200 to 350 A.D.*

A.D. before the year

The Spanish legions, under the leadership of Galba, conquered Rome in *A.D. 68.*

5-4. Standard Units of Measure

Common units of measure such as distance, length, temperature, volume, and weight are usually spelled out. They may be abbreviated, however, when space is limited; for example, on invoices, packing slips, and other business forms. In abbreviating units of measure, place periods after one-word abbreviations. However, in abbreviations consisting of more than one word, omit the periods.

correspondence

All perishable goods shipped over *100 miles* should be kept below *40 degrees Fahrenheit.*

forms, one-word abbreviations

12 ft. 2 in. (12 feet 2 inches)   *3 lb. 2 oz.* (3 pounds 2 ounces)

forms, multiple-word abbreviations

80 wpm (80 words per minute)   *55 mph* (55 miles per hour)

5-5. Metric Units of Measure

a. In regular business correspondence metric units of measurement are generally written out. However, on business forms and tables and in scientific and technical writing, they are often abbreviated. These abbreviations are written without periods. Use the same form for the singular and plural. Common abbreviations for measurements related to distance, weight, and volume follow.

prefixes

deci	*d* (1/10)	deka	*da* (× 10)
centi	*c* (1/100)	hecto	*h* (× 100)
milli	*m* (1/1000)	kilo	*k* (× 1000)

common units of measure

meter	*m*	centimeter	*cm*
gram	*g*	kilogram	*kg*
liter	*l*	milliliter	*ml*

square meter	*sq m*
cubic centimeter	*cu cm*

b. The abbreviation for *liter* is a lowercase *l*, but it is often typed with a capital *L*, since on many typewriters the lowercase letter "l" and numeral "1" (one) are typed with the same key. Therefore, to avoid confusion, the capital *L* is used instead.

1 *L* milk   *but*   1 *ml* vaccine (abbreviation is clear)

c. Temperatures in the metric system are expressed on the Celsius scale. This term is abbreviated *C*.

37°*C*   25°*C*

d. Express abbreviations relating to kilometers per hour with a diagonal.

The maximum speed limit on this highway is *90 km/h* (55 mph).

Slow down to *40 km/h* (25 mph) in the school crossing zone.

5–6. Business and General Terms

a. When the word *number* is not followed by a numeral, spell it out. The abbreviation *No.,* however, is used when a numeral directly follows the term, unless the term begins the sentence.

The stock *number* of the item you requested is *No. 4–862.*

Please ship us three *Model No. 17A* electric motors.

Number 18–A part is no longer stocked in our warehouse.

b. Commonly abbreviated business terms are generally typed in all capital letters with no spaces or periods separating the letters. A few business terms, when used in business correspondence, however, are written in lowercase letters separated by periods.

capital letters

PERT   GNP   LIFO

lowercase letters in correspondence

c.o.d.   f.o.b.

c. In giving telephone numbers with extensions, capitalize and abbreviate the word *extension* (Ext.).

You may reach me at 987-9281, Ext. 1201, any weekday between 10 and 11 a.m.

Please call me collect at (714) 365-3827, Ext. 248.

d. Some commonly abbreviated terms are derived from foreign expressions. They are generally typed in lowercase letters and are followed by a period at the close of each abbreviated word.

foreign abbreviations

e.g. (for example)	viz. (namely)
et al. (and others)	ibid. (in the same place)
i.e. (that is)	loc. cit. (in the place cited)
etc. (and so forth)	op. cit. (in the work cited)

5–7. Plurals

a. Most plural abbreviations are formed by adding *s* to the singular abbreviation. In some cases, however, abbreviations are the same in both singular and plural forms.

plural formed by adding "s"

hr., *hrs.*   mgr., *mgrs.*

singular and plural form identical

deg., *deg.*   ft., *ft.*

b. When an abbreviation consists of single letters, the plural is formed by adding *'s.*

plural formed by adding " 's"

c.o.d.*'s*   f.o.b.*'s*   IOU*'s*

5–8. Addresses and Geographical Expressions

a. For addresses in business correspondence, short terms such as *Street, Avenue,* and *Road* are spelled out. *Boulevard (Blvd.),* however, may be abbreviated if space is limited.

Ms. Lila Green
462 Olive *Avenue*
Iowa City, IA 52240

Mr. James F. Campenelli
1873 San Fernando Mission *Blvd.*
San Francisco, CA 94127

b. Terms indicating direction (*North, South, East, West*) within an address are spelled out. Compound directions such as *N.E.,* however, are abbreviated when they are used after the name of the street.

direction before street

851 *East* Lake Street

compound direction after street

7059 Capitol Avenue, *S.W.*

c. The post office at one time requested that on all mailings the names of states be abbreviated by using the official zip code designations. (They are typed in capital letters with no periods or spaces.) These two-letter state abbreviations are shown on pages 99–100.
Since optical scanning equipment no longer requires the use of the two-letter abbreviations, the full state name or the zip code designation may be used, depending on which form more nearly balances with the other lines of the address.

zip code designation

Mrs. Marjory Clark, PLS
Los Angeles Pierce College
6201 Winnetka Avenue
Woodland Hills, *CA* 91371

state spelled out fully

Fielder Publishing Company
9836 West Seventh Avenue
Ridgewood, *New Jersey* 07451

d.   A period is placed after each abbreviated word in geographical abbreviations. Only with the two-letter state abbreviations recommended by the U.S. Post Office Department are the periods omitted.

capital letters

U.S.A. (United States of America)

capital and lowercase letters

So. Nev. (Southern Nevada)

post office abbreviation
MT (Montana)

5–9. Abbreviation Format

a.   Capitalization of abbreviations is generally governed by the format of the original word or words. Proper nouns are always capitalized, while common nouns generally appear in lowercase letters.

capital letters

His father is a member of the *AFL-CIO.*

lowercase letters

Please send the order *c.o.d.*

b.   Abbreviations that appear in all capital letters are generally typed without periods or spaces. Geographic expressions and academic degrees, however, are typed with periods but no spaces. Initials in a person's name are typed with both periods and spaces.

general rule—no periods and no spaces

We heard the news from an *NBC* reporter.

Be sure to turn your dial to *KBIG* for beautiful music.

geographical expressions—periods with no spaces

Their travel agency sponsored several trips to the *U.S.S.R.* last summer.

We will return to the *U.S.* next spring.

academic degrees—periods with no spaces

Mr. Fujimoto was granted an *M.A.* in business last June.

Jane Hughes, *Ph.D.*, was awarded the position.

initials—periods and spaces

Please deliver this report to Ms. *J. T.* Kelly.

Only Gerald *H.* Monroe applied for the position.

c. In lowercase abbreviations a period is generally placed after each letter or group of letters representing a word, and there is no space between letters and periods in compound abbreviations. Exceptions include the abbreviations of metric measurements and compound abbreviations representing "measures per time."

general rule—periods

c.o.d. (collect on delivery)   *mgr.* (manager)
a.m. (ante meridiem)   *qt.* (quart)
ft. (foot or feet)   *amt.* (amount)

metric measurements—no periods

mm   ml   cm   kg

measures per time—no periods

rpm   wam   wpm

d. If an abbreviation containing a period falls at the end of a sentence, only one period is needed. In sentences ending with question marks or exclamation marks, place the mark directly after the period.

period

The hotel clerk awakened Mr. Sykiski at *8 a.m.*

question mark

Did you send the order *c.o.d.?*

exclamation mark

The plane was three hours late in arriving in the *U.S.A.!*

5–10. Commonly Used Abbreviations

Abbreviations of Common Business Terms

Term	Abbreviation	Term	Abbreviation
account	acct.	amount	amt.
accounts payable	a/p, A/P	*anno Domini*	A.D.
accounts		answer	ans.
receivable	a/r, A/R	*ante meridiem*	a.m.
advertisement	advt., ad	approximately	approx.
affidavit	afft.	assistant	asst., ass't.

Abbreviations of Common Business Terms (continued)

Term	Abbreviation	Term	Abbreviation
association	assn., assoc.	inch	in.
attention	attn.	incorporated	Inc.
attorney	atty.	insurance	ins.
audiovisual	AV	intelligence	
avenue	ave.	quotient	IQ
average	av., avg.	interest	int.
balance	bal.	inventory	invt.
before Christ	B.C.	invoice	inv.
bill of lading	B/L	limited	ltd.
bill of sale	B/S	manager	mgr.
brothers	bros.	manufacturing	mfg.
building	bldg.	memorandum	memo
bushel	bu.	merchandise	mdse.
by way of	via	minute	min.
capital	cap.	miscellaneous	misc.
carbon copy	cc, CC	Mister	Mr.
care of	c/o	Misters	Messrs.
carton	ctn.	Mistress	Mrs.
Celsius	C	month	mo.
charge	chg.	net weight	nt. wt.
collect (cash)		number	No.
on delivery	c.o.d., COD	okay	OK
commission	comm.	organization	org.
company	co.	original	orig.
corporation	corp.	ounce	oz.
cubic	cu.	overdraft	o.d., OD
department	dept.	package	pkg.
discount	disc.	page, pages	p., pp.
division	div.	paid	pd.
dozen	doz., dz.	pair	pr.
each	ea.	parcel post	p.p., PP
enclosure	enc., encl.	pint	pt.
esquire	esq.	*post meridiem*	p.m.
expense	exp.	post office	P.O.
extension	Ext.	postscript	P.S., PS
Fahrenheit	F	pound	lb.
foot, feet	ft.	president	pres.
forward	fwd.	profit and loss	P & L, P/L
free on board	f.o.b., FOB	public relations	PR
freight	frt.	purchase order	P.O., PO
gallon	gal.	quart	qt.
gross	gr.	quarter	qtr.
gross national		quire	qr.
product	GNP	railway	ry.
hour	hr.	ream, reams	rm.
hundredweight	cwt.	received	recd.
identification		respond, if you	
data	ID	please	R.S.V.P., RSVP

Abbreviations of Common Business Terms (continued)

Term	Abbreviation	Term	Abbreviation
returned	retd.	treasurer	treas.
rural free		very important	
delivery	RFD	person	VIP
secretary	sec., secy.,	vice-president	V.P.
	sec'y.	volume	vol.
section	sect.	week	wk.
shipment	shpt.	weight	wt.
supplement	supp.	yard	yd.
television	TV	year	yr.

Abbreviations of States and Territories

State or Territory	Standard Abbreviation	Two-Letter Abbreviation
Alabama	Ala.	AL
Alaska	Alas.	AK
Arizona	Ariz.	AZ
Arkansas	Ark.	AR
California	Calif.	CA
Canal Zone	C.Z.	CZ
Colorado	Colo.	CO
Connecticut	Conn.	CT
Delaware	Del.	DE
District of Columbia	D.C.	DC
Florida	Fla.	FL
Georgia	Ga.	GA
Guam		GU
Hawaii		HI
Idaho		ID
Illinois	Ill.	IL
Indiana	Ind.	IN
Iowa		IA
Kansas	Kans.	KS
Kentucky	Ky.	KY
Louisiana	La.	LA
Maine		ME
Maryland	Md.	MD
Massachusetts	Mass.	MA
Michigan	Mich.	MI
Minnesota	Minn.	MN
Mississippi	Miss.	MS
Missouri	Mo.	MO
Montana	Mont.	MT
Nebraska	Nebr.	NE
Nevada	Nev.	NV
New Hampshire	N.H.	NH
New Jersey	N.J.	NJ

5

Abbreviations of States and Territories (continued)

State or Territory	Standard Abbreviation	Two-Letter Abbreviation
New Mexico	N. Mex.	NM
New York	N.Y.	NY
North Carolina	N.C.	NC
North Dakota	N. Dak.	ND
Ohio		OH
Oklahoma	Okla.	OK
Oregon	Oreg.	OR
Pennsylvania	Pa., Penna.	PA
Puerto Rico	P.R.	PR
Rhode Island	R.I.	RI
South Carolina	S.C.	SC
South Dakota	S. Dak.	SD
Tennessee	Tenn.	TN
Texas	Tex.	TX
Utah		UT
Vermont	Vt.	VT
Virgin Islands	V.I.	VI
Virginia	Va.	VA
Washington	Wash.	WA
West Virginia	W. Va.	WV
Wisconsin	Wis.	WI
Wyoming	Wyo.	WY

Two-Letter Abbreviations for Canadian Provinces

Canadian Province	Abbreviation
Alberta	AB
British Columbia	BC
Labrador	LB
Manitoba	MB
New Brunswick	NB
Newfoundland	NF
Northwest Territories	NT
Nova Scotia	NS
Ontario	ON
Prince Edward Island	PE
Quebec	PQ
Saskatchewan	SK
Yukon Territory	YT

Contractions

5–11. Contractions

a. Contractions are similar to abbreviations in that they are shortened forms. Unlike abbreviations, however, contractions always contain an apostrophe to indicate where letters have been omitted. The use of single-word contractions is generally limited to business forms and tables. Some common single-word contractions follow:

ack'd (acknowledged)   rec't (receipt)
ass't (assistant)   sec'y (secretary)
gov't (government)   '79 (1979)
nat'l (national)

b. A second kind of contraction occurs with verb forms. By using an apostrophe to indicate where letters have been omitted, two words may be combined into one. The use of verb contractions is generally limited to informal business writing. A sampling of commonly used verb contractions follows:

aren't	(are not)	I've	(I have)
didn't	(did not)	that's	(that is)
doesn't	(does not)	there's	(there is)
don't	(do not)	they're	(they are)
hasn't	(has not)	wasn't	(was not)
she's	(she is)	we'll	(we will)
I'll	(I will)	who's	(who is)
isn't	(is not)	won't	(will not)
it's	(it is)	wouldn't	(would not)
let's	(let us)	you're	(you are)

5

6
literary and artistic titles

Literary and Artistic Titles Solution Finder

6

Titles

6–1. Published Works

a. Underline or place in all capital letters the titles of published books, magazines, newspapers, and pamphlets. In underlined titles, capitalize the first letter of the principal words in the title. Articles *(a, an, the),* conjunctions *(and, but, or, nor),* and prepositions with fewer than four letters *(of, in, on, to, for)* are not capitalized unless they appear at the beginning or end of the title.

book

A copy of The Random House Dictionary of the English Language arrived yesterday.

magazine

Have you read the latest issue of BETTER HOMES AND GARDENS?

newspaper

An article in yesterday's Wall Street Journal discussed sales trends in our industry.

pamphlet

Your Attitude Is Showing is a publication that should be distributed to our new employees.

b. Place in quotation marks the titles of chapters, sections, lessons, and other such subdivisions of published books or pamphlets. Capitalize the first letter of the principal words in the title.

chapter in a book

The final chapter, "Application of Word Processing Procedures," contributed immeasurably to the success of Office Systems and Management.

section in a pamphlet

Please review the section "Filling out the Application" before you apply for a job.

c. Place in quotation marks the titles of articles, regular features, or columns in magazines and newspapers. Capitalize the first letter of the principal words in the title.

article in a magazine

Did you see "Indoor Gardening" in last month's issue of Ladies' Home Journal?

column in a newspaper

Potter's "Financial Outlook" predicted a rising stock market during the next quarter.

d. Capitalize the first letter of subdivisions such as preface, contents, appendix, and index when they refer to a specific work.

The rule for punctuating words in a series can be found in the Appendix.

6–2. Unpublished Works

Place the titles of unpublished manuscripts, reports, theses, and dissertations in quotation marks. Capitalize the first letter of the principal words in the title.

title of report

Copies of "Report on Progress in Areas of Public Concern" were distributed to the board members last week.

6–3. Artistic Works

Place in quotation marks the titles of movies, television and radio shows, plays, musicals, operas, poems, songs, paintings, essays, lectures, and sermons. Capitalize the first letter of the principal words in the title.

movie

"Gone With the Wind" is a movie classic that still attracts thousands.

lecture

Dr. Zimmer's dynamic presentation, "Politics and Education," was concluded with a challenge the audience could not overlook.

television series

Reruns of "I Love Lucy" still entertain today's children.

Punctuation

6–4. Punctuation Format

a. Titles of literary and artistic works are often used in appositive expressions; that is, they are used to rename a previously mentioned noun. In cases where the title is not needed to identify the work, set it off from the rest of the sentence with commas. Where the title is needed for identification, no commas are used.

title unnecessary to determine which article

His latest article, "Marketing Changes in the Automotive Industry," recommended a startling departure from current policies.

title necessary to determine which book

The book Daisies Forever should soon make the best-seller list.

b.   Question marks appearing in quoted titles are placed inside the closing quotation mark. If the question mark in a title appears at the end of the sentence, no other form of punctuation is required.

statement

The play "Where is John?" opened last night.

statement

We saw the play "Where is John?"

question

Have you seen the play "Where is John?"

7
words often misused and confused

All entries in this chapter are in alphabetical order.

A/An

A (used before a word beginning with a consonant sound or a long ū sound)—Please call
a repairman to fix the typewriter. A union representative met with us yesterday.
An (used before a word beginning with a vowel sound other than the long ū sound)—
Please make an appointment for me with Miss Carlson.

A while/Awhile

A while (used as a noun meaning "a short time")—He will be here in a while.
Awhile (used as an adverb meaning "a short time")—He left awhile ago.

Accede/Exceed

Accede (to agree or consent)—I will accede to your wishes.
Exceed (to surpass a limit)—Many accidents occur when people exceed the speed limit.

Accept/Except

Accept (to take or receive)—Yes, I will be glad to accept your check.
Except (to leave out or exclude)—All orders have been delivered except Mr. Reed's.

Access/Excess

Access (admittance or approachability)—Everyone in the office should have access to
the files.
Excess (beyond ordinary limits; a surplus)—At the end of the day, all excess materials
should be stored.

Ad/Add

Ad (abbreviated form of advertisement)—We filled most of our personnel needs by
running an ad in the local newspaper.
Add (to increase by uniting or joining)—The new computer will add to the efficiency of the
office staff.

Adapt/Adept/Adopt

Adapt (to adjust or modify)—We must adapt ourselves to new situations.
Adept (skilled)—She is very adept at taking and transcribing dictation.
Adopt (to take and follow as one's own)—We will adopt Mrs. Williams' proposal.

Add: see Ad.

Addition/Edition

Addition (the process of uniting or joining)—The addition of more floor space is necessary to meet the increased production quotas.
Edition (a particular version of printed material)—Only the second edition of this book is
available now.

Adept: see Adapt.

Adherence/Adherents
Adherence (a steady attachment or loyalty)—A strict *adherence* to all safety procedures is required of all personnel.
Adherents (loyal supporters or followers)—There are many *adherents* to the space program and its importance to mankind.

Adopt: see Adapt.

Advice/Advise
Advice (a suggestion, an opinion, or a recommendation)—He would have avoided the problem if he had followed our *advice*.
Advise (to counsel or recommend)—We had to *advise* her not to sign the contract in its present form.

Affect/Effect
Affect v. (to influence or change)—Large pay raises throughout the country cannot help but *affect* the rate of inflation. Increased costs will *affect* our pricing policies on all merchandise.
Effect v. (to bring about or accomplish)—Our government plans to *effect* a change in the rate of inflation by tightening bank credits. Mrs. Hardy plans to *effect* a change in our personnel practices.
Effect n. (a result or consequence)—Inflation usually has a negative *effect* on our economy. The new vacation policy had no apparent *effect* on company morale.

7

Allowed/Aloud
Allowed (permitted)—Passengers are *allowed* 40 pounds of baggage aboard transcontinental flights.
Aloud (to speak audibly)—The message was read *aloud* so all could hear.

All ready/Already
All ready (all are prepared)—We are *all ready* to initiate the new procedure.
Already (by or before this time)—The time on the parking meter has *already* lapsed.

All right/Alright
All right (approving or agreeable)—It is *all right* with the company if people wish to continue working after age sixty-five.
Alright (an informal spelling of *all right* that is not appropriate for business writing).

All together/Altogether
All together (everyone in a group)—We must work *all together* if the company is to survive this crisis.
Altogether (wholly; entirely)—*Altogether* there are 20 families signed up for the company picnic.

Allude/Elude
Allude (to mention or refer to)—I *allude* to the fact that the popularity of small cars has increased in recent years.

Elude (to evade or escape)—The halfback was able to *elude* his pursuers through fancy footwork.

Allusion/Delusion/Illusion
Allusion (an indirect reference)—Several people made *allusions* to Mr. Reed's apparent laziness.
Delusion (a false belief)—He was under the *delusion* that no one liked him.
Illusion (a false image or misconception)—We were all under the *illusion* that the new equipment would enable us to reduce our office staff.

All ways/Always
All ways (by all methods)—We must try *all ways* possible to solve the problem.
Always (at all times; continually)—Our company is *always* on the lookout for a good secretary.

Almost/Most
Almost (an adverb meaning nearly)—Our company *almost* reached its sales quota this year.
Most (an adjective or subject complement meaning the greatest in amount or number)—Ellen Reynolds had the *most* votes in the election.

Aloud: see Allowed.

Already: see All ready.

Alright: see All right.

Altar/Alter
Altar (a structure used for worship)—The wedding flowers made the *altar* look particularly beautiful.
Alter (to change)—The plane had to *alter* its altitude to avoid hitting the mountain.

Altogether: see All together.

Always: see All ways.

Among/Between
Among (refers to more than two persons or things)—Distribute the supplies equally *among* the three departments.
Between (refers to two persons or things)—The final selection for the position is *between* Ms. McCreery and Mr. Muha.

Amount/Number
Amount (indicates mass items that cannot be counted and singular nouns)—A great *amount* of food was wasted because of the power failure.
Number (indicates items that can be counted and plural nouns)—A *number* of errors appear in this letter.

An: see A.

Annual/Annul
Annual (yearly)—The *annual* report of the company will be published next week.
Annul (to void or abolish)—We had to *annul* the contract because of legal complications.

Any one/Anyone
Any one (any one person or thing in a group, always followed by "of")—Please hand me *any one* of those pencils.
Anyone (any person)—We will hire *anyone* who can type 40 words a minute accurately.

Any way/Anyway
Any way (any method)—Is there *any way* we can reach you while you are on vacation?
Anyway (in any case)—Considering the low bids of our competitors, I don't believe we would have received the contract *anyway.*

Appraise/Apprise
Appraise (to estimate)—Before the merger, we hired an outside firm to *appraise* our assets.
Apprise (to inform or notify)—I will *apprise* Janet of the situation and obtain her reaction.

As/Like
As (used as a conjunction at the beginning of a clause)—I will get the material to you by Friday *as* I promised.
Like (used when the sentence requires a preposition)—I have never met anyone *like* him.

Ascent/Assent
Ascent (rising or going up)—The recent *ascent* of stock market prices is an encouraging sign.
Assent (to agree or admit as true)—Everyone at the meeting will surely *assent* to the plan.

Assistance/Assistants
Assistance (help or aid)—The project could not have been completed without your *assistance.*
Assistants (people who assist a superior)—The staffing report indicates that the general manager should have three *assistants.*

Assure/Ensure/Insure
Assure (to promise; to make a positive declaration)—I *assure* you that the loan will be paid back on time.
Ensure (to secure or make certain)—The loan will *ensure* the completion of the project.
Insure (to protect against loss)—We *insure* all our facilities against earthquake damage.

Attendance/Attendants
Attendance (being present or attending)—All members of the committee must be in *attendance* before the meeting can be called to order.

113

Attendants (one who attends with or to others)—The *attendants* had a difficult time parking all the cars for such a large crowd.

Awhile: see A while.

Bad/Badly
Bad (an adjective or subject complement used after such intransitive verbs as *feel* or *look*)—I feel *bad* that your request for a transfer cannot be granted.
Badly (an adverb)—We *badly* need more personnel if the survey is to be completed on time.

Bail/Bale
Bail (security)—*Bail* in this case was set at $1,500.
Bale (a large bundle)—One *bale* of used clothing was lost in transit.

Bare/Bear
Bare (uncovered, plain, or mere)—I had time to give him only the *bare* facts connected with the problem.
Bear (to carry or bring forth)—Unfortunately, he had to *bear* the brunt of the losses.

Beside/Besides
Beside (by the side of)—Please put the new file *beside* the one in the corner.
Besides (in addition to)—Who else *besides* Ms. Graham was awarded a bonus?

7

Between: see Among.

Biannual/Biennial
Biannual (occurring twice a year)—The *biannual* meeting of the stockholders will be held next week.
Biennial (occurring once every two years)—The *biennial* meeting of the society was canceled this year.

Billed/Build
Billed (charged for goods or services)—You will be *billed* on the 10th of each month.
Build (to construct)—We plan to *build* a new plant in Texas.

Bolder/Boulder
Bolder (more fearless or daring)—The board feels we need a *bolder* person as president.
Boulder (a large rock)—The damage to the tire was caused by a *boulder* in the road.

Build: see Billed.

Can/May
Can (the ability to do something)—Pauline *can* type and take dictation.
May (permission)—Yes, you *may* take a day's vacation tomorrow.

Capital/Capitol

Capital n. (a city in which the official seat of government is located; the wealth of an individual or firm)—The *capital* of Wisconsin is Madison. Much of our *capital* is tied up in equipment.

Capital adj. (a crime punishable by death; foremost in importance)—Treason in many countries is a *capital* crime. Her suggestion for improving our credit system was a *capital* idea.

Capitol n. (a building used by the U.S. Congress; a building in which a state legislature convenes)—The tour of the *capitol* was very interesting.

Census/Senses

Census (an official count of a country's population)—The United States takes a *census* every ten years.

Senses (a clear state of mind)—He finally came to his *senses* concerning his appearance after he had interviewed for several job openings.

Cereal/Serial

Cereal (a breakfast food made from grain)—The diet called for a serving of wheat *cereal*.

Serial (arranged in a series)—The *serial* numbers of all our vehicles should be on file.

Choose/Chose

Choose (to select or make a choice)—We don't know whom he will *choose* for his executive secretary.

Chose (past tense of "choose")—He *chose* Ms. Randall to be his executive secretary.

Cite/Sight/Site

Cite (to quote or mention)—He can *cite* many authorities who have studied the problem.

Sight (to see or take aim; a view)—The hills above our home are a beautiful *sight* in the spring.

Site (a location)—This is a perfect *site* for the housing project.

Coarse/Course

Coarse (rough texture)—This material is too *coarse* for our use.

Course (a particular direction or route; part of a meal; a unit of learning)—We are now committed to a *course* of action that will hopefully solve the problem.

Collision/Collusion

Collision (a crash)—No one was hurt in the *collision*.

Collusion (an agreement to defraud)—No one suspected them of *collusion*.

Complement/Compliment

Complement (that which completes or makes perfect)—The color of the trim will *complement* the color of the walls.

Compliment (to praise or flatter)—Mr. Rose did *compliment* me on the fine job I had done.

Confidant/Confident

Confidant (a trusted friend)—He has been his closest *confidant* for years.

Confident (sure of oneself)—Mrs. Allan was *confident* she would get the position.

Conscience/Conscious
Conscience (the faculty of knowing right from wrong)—In the last analysis, it was his *conscience* that made him release the funds.
Conscious (aware or mentally awake)—Yes, we are *conscious* of the fact that a new product similar to ours is on the market.

Console/Consul
Console (a cabinet)—The stereo was so popular because of its attractive *console.*
Consul (an official representing a foreign country)—Travel information can often be obtained by contacting the *consul* of the country one wishes to visit.

Continual/Continuous
Continual (a regular or frequent occurrence)—These *continual* telephone calls are disrupting my regular routine.
Continuous (without interruption or cessation)—His *continuous* humming was disturbing to everyone in the office.

Cooperation/Corporation
Cooperation (working together)—The full *cooperation* of all employees is needed to reduce our high rate of absenteeism.
Corporation (one type of business organization)—We are looking into the possibility of forming a *corporation.*

Correspondence/Correspondents
Correspondence (letters or other written communications)—Our last *correspondence* from Mr. Flores was on October 14.
Correspondents (letter writers or news reporters)—Our African *correspondents* report that several countries are now having severe food shortages.

Council/Counsel
Council (a governing body)—We will present the proposal to the *council* in the morning.
Counsel (to give advice; advice)—He received good *counsel* from his advisors.

Course: see Coarse.

Credible/Creditable
Credible (believable or reliable)—The reason she gave for her long absence was a *credible* one.
Creditable (bringing honor or praise)—The new time-saving device developed by Ms. Cohen is a *creditable* feat of which she can be proud.

Decent/Descent/Dissent
Decent (in good taste; proper)—The *decent* thing would have been for the salesperson to apologize.
Descent (moving downward)—The view of the city was breathtaking as the plane started its *descent* into the airport.
Dissent (to differ or disagree)—There was no *dissent* among the council members concerning the resolution to expand our parking facilities.

Defer/Differ
Defer (to put off or delay)—They decided to *defer* the project until next spring.
Differ (to vary or disagree)—Doctors *differ* in their opinions as to the best treatment for this particular virus.

Deference/Difference
Deference (yielding to someone else's wishes)—In *deference* to the shoppers' requests, the store remained open until 9 p.m. during the summer months.
Difference (state of being different; dissimilarity)—There is little *difference* between the two products.

Delusion: see Allusion.

Deprecate/Depreciate
Deprecate (to disapprove or downgrade)—His speech did nothing but *deprecate* the present zoning system.
Depreciate (to lessen the value)—We will *depreciate* this new equipment over a ten-year period.

Descent: see Decent.

Device/Devise
Device (an invention or mechanism)—The *device* worked perfectly during the demonstration.
Devise (to think out or plan)—It was not easy to *devise* an overtime plan that would be equitable for everyone.

7

Dew/Do/Due
Dew (drops of moisture)—The heavy morning *dew* caused her to delay the flight.
Do (to perform or bring about)—We must *do* everything possible to ship the order by June 17.
Due (immediately payable)—All payments are *due* by the 10th of each month.

Differ: see Defer.

Difference: see Deference.

Disapprove/Disprove
Disapprove (to withhold approval)—The boss will *disapprove* any plan that is not properly justified.
Disprove (to prove false)—We must *disprove* the rumor that we are cutting back production next month.

Disburse/Disperse
Disburse (to pay out)—A new system has been devised to *disburse* commissions more rapidly.
Disperse (to scatter)—The plan to *disperse* branch offices throughout the state is not economically feasible.

117

Disprove: see Disapprove.

Dissent: see Decent.

Do: see Dew.

Due: see Dew.

Edition: see Addition.

Effect: see Affect.

Elicit/Illicit
Elicit (to draw out or bring forth)—The speaker had a difficult time trying to *elicit* responses from the audience.
Illicit (unlawful)—He was cited for *illicit* business practices.

Elude: see Allude.

Emigrate/Immigrate
Emigrate (to move to another country)—Many Cubans decided to *emigrate* to the United States after Castro came to power.
Immigrate (to enter a country)—The United States welcomed those Cubans who *immigrated* after Castro came to power.

Eminent/Imminent
Eminent (prominent; distinguished)—Mr. Mendez is an *eminent* authority on labor relations.
Imminent (impending; likely to occur)—There is *imminent* danger of equipment breakdown unless periodic service checks are made.

Ensure: see Assure.

Envelop/Envelope
Envelop (to wrap, surround, or conceal)—The chief said his men would *envelop* the fire by morning.
Envelope (a container for a letter)—Please send me your answer in the return *envelope* provided for your convenience.

Every day/Everyday
Every day (each day)—I will call you *every day* and give you a status report on the new project,
Everyday (ordinary)—Sales meetings are an *everyday* occurrence in this office.

Every one/Everyone
Every one (each person in a group)—*Every one* of our secretaries can run our word processing equipment.

Everyone (all people in a group)—*Everyone* is expected to be on time for the stockholders' meeting.

Exceed: see Accede.

Except: see Accept.

Excess: see Access.

Expand/Expend
Expand (to enlarge)—The plan to *expand* our storage facilities was approved.
Expend (to use up or pay out)—We must be careful not to *expend* too much time on minor problems.

Expansive/Expensive
Expansive (capable of expanding; extensive)—An *expansive* commercial development is planned for this area.
Expensive (costly)—The consultant's recommendations were too *expensive* to implement.

Expend: see Expand.

Expensive: see Expansive.

7

Explicit/Implicit
Explicit (expressed clearly)—The letter gives *explicit* instructions for assembling the new machine.
Implicit (implied)—By reading between the lines, you can discern an *implicit* appeal for additional funds.

Farther/Further
Farther (a greater distance)—The trip to the plant is *farther* than I thought.
Further (additional; to help forward)—Refer to my July 8 memo for *further* details.

Fewer/Less
Fewer (items that can be counted and plural nouns)—We had *fewer* sales this month.
Less (mass items that cannot be counted and singular nouns)—You will get by with *less* work if you follow my suggestions.

Finally/Finely
Finally (in the end)—The missing part was *finally* delivered.
Finely (elegantly or delicately)—We all admired the *finely* embroidered tapestry.

Flagrant/Fragrant
Flagrant (glaring; scandalous)—His behavior was a *flagrant* violation of company rules.
Fragrant (sweet smelling)—She received a *fragrant* bouquet of flowers from the staff.

Flew/Flu/Flue
Flew (past tense of "fly")—The plane *flew* to the West Coast in record time.
Flu (abbreviated form of influenza)—Over 30 percent of our employees are absent because of the *flu.*
Flue (a duct in a chimney)—Unless the *flue* is open, smoke cannot escape through the chimney.

Formally/Formerly
Formally (in a formal manner)—At our next meeting you will be *formally* initiated into the organization.
Formerly (in the past)—She was *formerly* the president of a large community college.

Former/Latter
Former (first of two things or belonging to an earlier time)—As a *former* employee, Grace Noonan is always welcome at our yearly company picnic.
Latter (second of two things or nearer to the end)—Of the two proposals the *latter* one seems more workable than the former one.

Forth/Fourth
Forth (forward)—The speaker asked that his illustrations be brought *forth.*
Fourth (a numeric term)—The *fourth* member of our group never arrived.

Fragrant: see Flagrant.

Further: see Farther.

Good/Well
Good (an adjective that describes a noun or pronoun)—Mr. Collins writes *good* letters.
Well (an adverb that describes a verb, an adjective, or another adverb; a person's well being and health)—Miss Farley takes dictation very *well*. My secretary did not look *well* today.

He/Him/Himself
He (the subject of a clause or a complement pronoun)—*He* is the one I interviewed for the job. It was *he* who asked for an appointment.
Him (a direct object, an indirect object, or an object of a preposition)—The president asked *him* to head the project. Mrs. Roberts gave *him* the results of the study yesterday. The choice is between you and *him.*
Himself (a reflexive pronoun used to emphasize a noun or as an object)—He had to see for *himself* what the problem was.

Hear/Here
Hear (to perceive by the ear)—Yes, I can *hear* you clearly.
Here (in this place or at this point)—Install the telephone *here.*

Her/She/Herself
Her (a direct object, an indirect object, or an object of a preposition)—When Paulette

arrived, Mr. Shultz asked *her* for the information. Barbara offered *her* a chair. Please send a request for payment to *her.*

She (the subject of a clause or a complement pronoun)—*She* went to lunch about 15 minutes ago. It was *she* who typed the memorandum.

Herself (a reflexive pronoun used to emphasize a noun or as an object)—Wendy wrote and dictated the entire audit report *herself.*

Here: see Hear.

Herself: see Her.

Him: see He.

Himself: see He.

Hoard/Horde
Hoard (to store or accumulate for future use)—Please do not *hoard* supplies.
Horde (a multitude)—A *horde* of people were waiting for the doors to open.

Holy/Wholly
Holy (sacred)—This place is considered *holy* by some people.
Wholly (completely)—Do you agree *wholly* with the committee's recommendations?

Horde: see Hoard.

Hypercritical/Hypocritical
Hypercritical (excessively critical)—Many believed him to be *hypercritical* of new employees.
Hypocritical (falsely pretending)—No one likes *hypocritical* people.

I/Me/Myself
I (a subject of a clause or a complement pronoun)—*I* finished the report last night. It was *I* who took the message.
Me (a direct object, an indirect object, or an object of a preposition)—They phoned *me* this morning. She gave *me* the report to edit. The company is sending the material to *me.*
Myself (a reflexive pronoun used to emphasize a noun or as an object)—I wrote the entire report *myself.*

Ideal/Idle/Idol
Ideal (perfect; model)—Your proposal outlines an *ideal* solution to the problem.
Idle (doing nothing)—The production line was *idle* for almost a week.
Idol (an object for religious worship; a revered person)—He is the *idol* of every teenager.

Illicit: see Elicit.

Illusion: see Allusion.

Immigrate: see Emigrate.

Imminent: see Eminent.

Implicit: see Explicit.

Imply/Infer
Imply (to suggest without stating)—Does that statement *imply* that I have made a mistake?
Infer (to reach a conclusion)—I cannot comment for fear people will *infer* the wrong thing.

Incidence/Incidents
Incidence (occurrence)—There has never been an *incidence* of theft within the company.
Incidents (events or episodes)—Four *incidents* occurred in which injuries resulted from faulty equipment.

Incite/Insight
Incite (to urge on or provoke action)—The speaker attempted to *incite* the audience to take action.
Insight (keen understanding)—His *insight* into the situation prevented a serious problem.

Indigenous/Indigent/Indignant
Indigenous (native of a particular region)—I believe that this metal is *indigenous* only to the Northwest.
Indigent (poor; needy)—My parents were *indigent* farmers.
Indignant (insulting; angry)—You should learn how to deal with *indignant* customers.

Infer: see Imply.

Insight: see Incite.

Insure: see Assure.

Interstate/Intrastate
Interstate (between states)—We are now involved in *interstate* commerce.
Intrastate (within a state)—This firm is primarily concerned with *intrastate* product sales.

Its/It's
Its (possessive form of "it")—The company had *its* stockholders' meeting last week.
It's (contraction of "it is")—*It's* a fact that our office is first in sales.

Later/Latter
Later (after the proper time)—The shipment arrived *later* than we had anticipated.
Latter (the second thing of two things mentioned)—Your *latter* suggestion is more likely to be adopted.

Lay/Lie

Lay (to put or place; a transitive verb that needs an object to complete its meaning; *lay, laid, laid,* and *laying* are the principal parts of this verb)—Please *lay* the message on my desk. I *laid* the message on your desk. I have *laid* several messages on your desk. We are *laying* the foundation for the new building today.

Lie (to recline; an intransitive verb that does not have an object; *lie, lay, lain,* and *lying* are the principal parts of this verb)—May I *lie* down? He *lay* in bed for two weeks recuperating from his accident. These papers have *lain* on your desk since Monday. She is *lying* down.

Lean/Lien

Lean (to rest against; to be inclined toward)—I believe the employees *lean* toward the first contract proposal.

Lien (a legal right or claim to property)—If he refuses to pay, we will be forced to obtain a *lien* on the property.

Leased/Least

Leased (rented property for a specified time period)—The building has been *leased* for three years.

Least (smallest; slightest; lowest)—This month we had the *least* profit for this year.

Less: see Fewer.

Lessee/Lesser/Lessor

Lessee (one to whom a lease is given)—As specified in the lease agreement, the *lessee* is responsible for the maintenance of the property.

Lesser (smaller or less important)—Although the decision was not wholly satisfactory, it was the *lesser* of the two evils.

Lessor (one who grants the lease)—The *lessor* is usually responsible for paying the utility costs of leased property.

7

Lessen/Lesson

Lessen (to make smaller)—She recommended we *lessen* our efforts in the manufacturing area.

Lesson (a unit of study; something from which one learns)—The experience was a good *lesson* in how miscommunication can cause problems.

Lesser: see Lessee.

Lessor: see Lessee.

Levee/Levy

Levee (the bank of a river or a boat landing)—The river overflowed the *levee*.

Levy (an order for payment)—To pay for the flood damage, the governor ordered a 1 percent *levy* on gasoline sales.

Liable/Libel

Liable (legally responsible; obligated)—The court ruled that the company was *liable* for the accident.

Libel (a false or damaging statement about another made in public)—He refused to include the statement in his speech because he feared he would be sued for *libel.*

Lie: see Lay.

Lien: see Lean.

Like: see As.

Local/Locale
Local (limited to a particular district)—Only persons living in the *local* area were interviewed.
Locale (a particular location)—This parcel is an ideal *locale* for the new plant.

Loose/Lose
Loose (not fastened, tight, or shut up)—A *loose* connection was the probable cause of the power failure.
Lose (to fail to keep; to mislay)—Please be careful not to *lose* this statement.

Marital/Marshal/Martial
Marital (pertaining to marriage)—Use *"marital* bliss" for the primary sales theme in your advertising copy.
Marshal (a military rank; the head of a ceremony)—He was asked to act as honorary *marshal* of the parade.
Martial (warlike; military)—A band played *martial* music at the concert.

May: see Can.

May be/Maybe
May be (a verb form)—This *may be* the last year we will be able to expand.
Maybe (an adverb meaning perhaps)—*Maybe* the new carpeting will reduce the noise level in the office.

Me: see I.

Medal/Meddle
Medal (a metal disk; an award in the form of a metal disk)—He should receive a *medal* for his efforts.
Meddle (to interfere)—It was an argument in which he dared not *meddle*.

Miner/Minor
Miner (a person who works in a mine)—He listed his last job as that of a *miner*.
Minor (a lesser thing; person under legal age)—It proved to be a *minor* matter.

Moral/Morale
Moral (pertaining to right and wrong; ethical)—She made the decision on a *moral* rather than on a practical basis.

7

Morale (a mental condition)—The announcement of a pay raise boosted the employee *morale*.

Most: see Almost.

Myself: see I.

Number: see Amount.

Ordinance/Ordnance
Ordinance (a local regulation)—The city passed an *ordinance* banning excessive noise after 10 p.m.
Ordnance (military weapons)—We should know by the end of the month whether we will receive the army *ordnance* contract.

Overdo/Overdue
Overdo (to exaggerate)—Exercise is healthful if one does not *overdo* it.
Overdue (late)—Your payment is 15 days *overdue*.

Pair/Pare/Pear
Pair (two of a kind; made of two corresponding parts)—The *pair* of gloves I bought for her birthday were too small.
Pare (to reduce in size or trim)—I hope you can *pare* this budget at least 15 percent.
Pear (a fruit)—He always eats a *pear* for breakfast.

Passed/Past
Passed (past tense or past participle of "pass," meaning to go by or circulate)—She *passed* around the announcement to everyone in the office.
Past (gone by or ended)—Our weak profit picture is all in the *past*.

Patience/Patients
Patience (calm perseverance)—It took great *patience* on her part to type the report without error.
Patients (people undergoing medical treatment)—I am one of Dr. Taylor's *patients*.

Peace/Piece
Peace (truce; tranquillity)—Since she began the project, she has not had one moment's *peace*.
Piece (a part of limited quantity)—Each of us had a *piece* of the birthday cake.

Pear: see Pair.

Persecute/Prosecute
Persecute (to harass persistently)—He is the type of person who wouldn't hesitate to *persecute* a colleague if it would be to his advantage.
Prosecute (to start legal proceedings against someone)—We are not sure whether or not the district attorney will *prosecute* the case.

Personal/Personnel
Personal (private; individual)—She is his *personal* secretary.
Personnel (employees)—All *personnel* are requested to work overtime until the inventory has been completed.

Perspective/Prospective
Perspective (a mental picture or outlook)—His *perspective* is distorted by greed.
Prospective (likely; expected)—We interviewed several *prospective* secretaries last week.

Piece: see Peace.

Precede/Proceed
Precede (to go before)—Mrs. Andrews' presentation will *precede* the main speaker's address.
Proceed (to go forward or continue)—Please *proceed* with your analysis of the financial statements.

Precedence/Precedents
Precedence (priority)—Please give *precedence* to Mr. Wilson's application for funds.
Precedents (things done or said that can be used as an example)—There are no *precedents* for this particular case.

Principal/Principle
Principal n. (a capital sum; a school official)—Both the *principal* and interest on the balance of the loan are due next month. As *principal* of Lindberg High School, Mrs. Brereton was proud that so many of its students continued on to college.
Principal adj. (highest in importance)—The *principal* reason we changed our promotion procedures was to encourage all our employees to try and upgrade themselves within the company.
Principle n. (an accepted rule of action; a basic truth or belief)—Her knowledge of accounting *principles* is questionable. Our country was founded on the *principle* that all men are created equal.

Proceed: see Precede.

Propose/Purpose
Propose (to suggest)—I *propose* that we borrow the money for the new equipment.
Purpose (a desired result)—The *purpose* of this meeting is to discuss ways in which sales can be increased.

Prosecute: see Persecute.

Prospective: see Perspective.

Purpose: see Propose.

Quiet/Quite

Quiet (peaceful; free from noise)—The *quiet* operation of this typewriter is one of its main sales features.

Quite (completely or actually)—The salespeople seem to be *quite* satisfied with the new commission plan.

Raise/Rise

Raise (to lift something up, increase in amount, gather together, or bring into existence; a transitive verb that needs an object to complete its meaning; *raise, raised, raised,* and *raising* are the principal parts of this verb)—Please do not *raise* your voice. We *raised* $200 for Ms. Morgan's retirement gift. He has *raised* our quota 30 percent during the last month. We are *raising* the money for his gift.

Rise (to go up or increase in value; an intransitive verb that does not have an object; *rise, rose, risen,* and *rising* are the principal parts of this verb)—One should *rise* when her honor enters the courtroom. The rocket *rose* 30,000 feet before it exploded. Our sales have *risen* for the third month in a row. Production is *rising* steadily since the new equipment has been installed.

Real/Really

Real (an adjective meaning great in amount or number)—The new word processing machine was a *real* help in getting out our monthly statements.

Really (an adverb meaning actually or truly)—Wilma Carroll *really* needed her vacation after the tax season was over.

Reality/Realty

Reality (that which is real; that which exists)—Our problem began when the manager would not face *reality* in negotiating with the employees.

Realty (real estate)—The last *realty* company that tried to sell my property could not find an interested buyer.

Receipt/Recipe

Receipt (a written acknowledgment for receiving goods or money)—No refunds can be made without a *receipt*.

Recipe (a set of instructions)—He has always kept secret the *recipe* for his delicious spaghetti sauce.

Residence/Residents

Residence (a dwelling)—This house has been her *residence* for the past twenty years.

Residents (people who reside in a dwelling)—One of the *residents* complained that the heater in her apartment does not work.

Respectfully/Respectively

Respectfully (used in the body or complimentary close of a letter to show high regard or respect for the reader)—We *respectfully* submit that the contract calls for all work to be completed by April 1.

Respectively (each in turn or in order)—Janice Jackson, Al Turnbull, and Gary Woods were first, second, and third prize winners, *respectively*.

Rise: see Raise.

Rote/Rout/Route
Rote (mechanical or repetitious learnings)—All of us had to learn the multiplication tables by *rote* memory.
Rout (a disorderly assembly or flight)—The game turned into a *rout* after the opposing team scored 30 points in the first quarter.
Route (a course taken in traveling from one point to another)—Most of our delivery *routes* had to be changed after they were studied by efficiency experts.

Scene/Seen
Scene (a place of an occurrence; an exhibition of anger)—The police arrived at the *scene* shortly after the guard telephoned them.
Seen (past participle of "to see")—The customer was not served because he was not *seen*.

Senses: see Census.

Serial: see Cereal.

Set/Sit
Set (to place or make solid; a transitive verb that generally needs an object to complete its meaning; *set, set, set,* and *setting* are the principal parts of this verb)—Please *set* the calculator on my desk. He *set* the clocks ahead for daylight saving time. I have *set* the times for your appointments this week. We are *setting* higher sales quotas this year.
Sit (to be seated or occupy a seat; an intransitive verb that does not have an object; *sit, sat, sat,* and *sitting* are the principal parts of this verb)—*Sit* here, Ms. Brown. I *sat* for an hour awaiting his return. He has *sat* in that chair all day watching television. If anyone calls, tell him I am *sitting* in on a meeting of all department heads.

Sew/So/Sow
Sew (to fasten by stitches with thread)—I can't find anyone who will *sew* a button on my coat.
So (in a way indicated; to that degree; therefore)—She was *so* upset over the incident that she accidentally tore the paper.
Sow (to scatter seed)—This machine can *sow* more seed than any 15 farmhands.

Shall/Will
Shall (used in formal writing when the first person is employed)—I *shall* give your request the utmost consideration.
Will (used with all three persons except in formal writing)—They *will* finish the project on time unless they run into bad weather conditions.

She: see Her.

Shear/Sheer
Shear (to cut, strip, or remove)—We had to *shear* off the bolts before we could remove the wheel.
Sheer (transparently thin; utterly; a steep incline)—The conference was a *sheer* waste of time.

Shone/Shown
Shone (past tense of "shine")—If only the flashing red lights had *shone* through the dense fog, the accident might have been avoided.
Shown (past participle of "show")—The filmstrip displaying our new products has been *shown* to the salespeople.

Should/Would
Should (used in formal writing when the first person is employed)—We *should* like you to return the completed application by Friday.
Would (used with all three persons except in formal writing)—She *would* be happy to work overtime if the report isn't finished.

Sight: see Cite.

Sit: see Set.

Site: see Cite.

So: see Sew.

Some/Somewhat
Some (an adjective or subject complement meaning an unknown amount)—The report revealed that we will have to make *some* changes when we move to the new facility.
Somewhat (an adverb meaning to some degree)—Most people feel our proposed budget is *somewhat* overly optimistic.

Some time/Sometime
Some time (a period of time)—It took *some time* for us to get used to coming to work an hour early.
Sometime (an indefinite time)—Your order should be delivered *sometime* next week.

Sow: see Sew.

Staid/Stayed
Staid (sedate; composed)—A more *staid* individual is needed to fill this position.
Stayed (past tense and past participle of "stay")—She *stayed* long after closing time to finish the report.

Stationary/Stationery
Stationary (not moving)—The table would not remain *stationary* while I typed.
Stationery (writing material)—Mr. Long wants this letter typed on his personal *stationery*.

Statue/Stature/Statute
Statue (a carved or molded image of someone or something)—Meet me in front of the *statue* of Lincoln.
Stature (the height of an object; status gained by attainment)—She is a person of great *stature* within the community.
Statute (law enacted by legislature)—There is a *statute* in this state that prohibits gambling in any form.

Stayed: see Staid.

Sure/Surely
Sure (an adjective or subject complement meaning certain or positive)—Nancy was *sure* she had made the right decision.
Surely (an adverb meaning certainly or undoubtedly)—The employees believed that they would *surely* get a raise this year.

Tare/Tear/Tier
Tare (the weight of goods after the weight of the container is deducted)—The *tare* cost of our merchandise has increased over 15 percent in one year.
Tear (to pull apart or rip)—The customer complained about a *tear* in the sweater she purchased.
Tier (things placed one above the other)—Our season tickets are on the third *tier* of the stadium.

Than/Then
Than (a conjunction used to show comparison)—Miss Espinoza had more experience *than* I in writing contract proposals.
Then (an adverb meaning at that time)—After a letter is typed, it should *then* be proofread carefully before it is removed from the typewriter.

That/Which
That (introduces a restrictive or essential subordinate clause)—Mr. Sparks said *that* this order must be shipped today. All animals *that* are found wandering in the streets will be impounded. This is the telephone *that* has been out of order since this morning.
Which (introduces a nonrestrictive or nonessential subordinate clause)—The security people recommend we acquire a watchdog, *which* would be kept inside the plant at night. Our new credit verification system, *which* will be installed next week, will cost over $50,000.

Their/There/They're
Their (the possessive form of "they")—It was *their* recommendation that we install the new computer system.
There (at that place or at that point)—Please be *there* promptly at ten o'clock in the morning.
They're (contraction of "they are")—Although most of the secretaries are new employees, *they're* exceptionally familiar with our operations.

Them/They
Them (a direct object, an indirect object, or an object of a preposition)—I asked *them* to please wait outside. I sent *them* a bill last week. I waited for *them* all morning.
They (subject of a clause or a complement pronoun)—*They* are meeting this afternoon. It was *they* who painted the office.

Then: see Than.

There: see Their.

They: see Them.

They're: see Their.

Threw/Through
Threw (past tense of "throw")—Mr. Hardy accidentally *threw* away the report on equipment purchases.
Through (in one end and out the other; over the surface of; the end of; during the period of; as a consequence of)—It will be a pleasure to give you a tour *through* the plant.

Tier: see Tare.

To/Too/Two
To (a preposition; the sign of an infinitive)—She wanted *to* see for herself the condition of the plant cafeteria.
Too (an adverb meaning also or to an excessive extent)—I was there *too*. Because the office was *too* noisy, I had a difficult time hearing you on the telephone.
Two (a number)—There was just too much work for the *two* of us to finish by five o'clock.

Us/We
Us (a direct object, an indirect object, or an object of a preposition)—The vice-president took *us* on a tour of the plant. The manager gave *us* a copy of the report. The company certainly did renovate the lounge for us.
We (the subject of a clause or a complement pronoun)—*We* have to catch a plane at 3 p.m. It was *we* who had to solve the problem.

7

Vain/Van/Vane/Vein
Vain (unduly proud or conceited)—Tom would be more popular with his fellow workers if he were not so *vain*.
Van (a covered truck)—Our *van* has a variety of uses within the company.
Vane (a thin plate used to show wind direction)—The weather *vane* indicated that the wind was coming from a westward direction.
Vein (a tubular vessel that carries blood to the heart)—She had difficulty finding a *vein* from which to obtain a blood sample.

Vary/Very
Vary (to change)—The new office manager said she would not request us to *vary* any procedures at the present time.
Very (extremely)—These figures are *very* difficult to type accurately.

Vein: see Vain.

Vice/Vise
Vice (immoral habit; personal fault)—Cigar smoking is his only *vice*.
Vise (a clamp; to hold or squeeze)—He shook my hand with a *vise*-like grip.

Waiver/Waver

Waiver (the relinquishment of a claim)—Please sign this *waiver* releasing the company of any responsibility for the injury.
Waver (to shake or fluctuate)—I believe he is beginning to *waver* concerning my request for an early vacation.

We: see Us.

Weather/Whether

Weather (the state of the atmosphere; to bear up against)—We are glad to learn that you were able to *weather* the high rate of employee turnover during the summer months.
Whether (an introduction of alternatives)—We will not know until next week *whether* or not our company will be awarded the contracts.

Well: see Good.

Whether: see Weather.

Which: see That.

Who/Whom

Who (the subject of a subordinate clause or a complement pronoun)—I was the one *who* asked you to attend. I cannot tell you *who* it was at the door.
Whom (a direct object, an indirect object, or an object of a preposition)—*Whom* have you hired as my assistant? He sent *whom* the book? Here is the address of the person with *whom* we met for legal assistance.

Wholly: see Holy.

Whom: see Who.

Who's/Whose

Who's (a contraction of "who is")—Please let me know *who's* taking over for her during August.
Whose (possessive form of "who")—He is the fellow *whose* position was abolished.

Will: see Shall.

Would: see Should.

Your/You're

Your (possessive form of "you")—*Your* secretary told me that you would invite the mayor to the reception.
You're (contraction of "you are")—So *you're* the one who has been trying to reach me.

8
GRAMMAR

Grammar Solution Finder

8

8

Nouns

8–1. Noun Plurals*

a. Most nouns form their plurals by adding *s*. However, nouns ending in *s, sh, ch, x,* or *z* form their plurals by adding *es*.

nouns adding "s"

account	accounts
executive	executives
letter	letters

nouns adding "es"

business	businesses
wish	wishes
branch	branches
tax	taxes
buzz	buzzes

b. Common nouns ending in *y* form the plural in one of two ways. If the letter preceding the *y* is a vowel, just add *s*. However, if the letter preceding the *y* is a consonant, drop the *y* and add *ies*.

"y" preceded by a vowel

attorney	attorneys
money	moneys
valley	valleys

"y" preceded by a consonant

company	companies
secretary	secretaries
reply	replies

c. Musical terms ending in *o* form the plural by adding *s*. Other common nouns ending in *o* may form the plural by adding *s* or *es*; the correct plural forms are shown in the dictionary.

The rules in this chapter are based on *Webster's New Collegiate Dictionary* (Springfield, Mass.: G. & C. Merriam Company, 1977).

*Noun plurals, other than those regular ones ending in *s* or *es*, are shown in the dictionary immediately after the singular form of the word.

8

musical terms

sopranos	concertos	cellos	solos

common nouns ending in "os"

zeros	mementos	dynamos	portfolios

common nouns ending in "oes"

cargoes	heroes	potatoes	embargoes

d. Nouns ending in *ff* form the plural by adding *s*. Nouns ending in just *f* or *fe* may add *s*, or they may drop the *f* or *fe* and add *ves*. The plurals of those nouns taking the irregular form by adding *ves* are shown in the dictionary. If the dictionary does not show the plural form, just add *s*.

plural nouns ending in "ffs"

sheriff	sheriffs
cliff	cliffs

plural nouns ending in "fs" or "fes"

proof	proofs
safe	safes

plural nouns ending in "ves"

wife	wives
half	halves

e. The plurals of proper nouns are formed by adding *s* or *es*. Those proper nouns ending in *s, sh, ch, x,* or *z* form the plural by adding *es*. All others form the plural by adding *s*.

proper noun plurals ending in "es"

Winters	Winterses
Bush	Bushes
Finch	Finches
Rodriguez	Rodriguezes
Bendix	Bendixes

proper noun plurals ending in "s"

Halby	Halbys
Dixon	Dixons
Wolf	Wolfs

8

137

f. Many nouns of foreign origin have both an English plural and a foreign plural. Consult your dictionary and use the one that appears first.

foreign nouns with English plurals

memorandum	memorandums
index	indexes
formula	formulas

foreign nouns with foreign plurals

alumna	alumnae
alumnus	alumni
criterion	criteria
curriculum	curricula
terminus	termini
datum	data

g. Some nouns form their plurals by changing letters within the word or adding letters other than *s* or *es*. These irregular plurals are shown in the dictionary.

tooth	teeth
man	men
child	children
mouse	mice
foot	feet
woman	women

h. Some nouns have the same form in both the singular and plural. Other nouns are always singular, and others are always plural.

nouns with same singular and plural form

fish	politics
scissors	measles
gross	series
Vietnamese	species
headquarters	deer

nouns always singular

news	mathematics
genetics	aeronautics

nouns always plural

earnings	proceeds
cattle	thanks

i. Hyphenated or open compound nouns containing a main word form their plurals

8

on the main words. Those hyphenated compounds not containing a main word and compound nouns that consist of only one word form the plural at the end.

plural formed on main word

personnel managers	sisters-in-law
leaves of absence	notaries public
lieutenant colonels	vice-presidents
attorneys-at-law	

plural formed on end word

follow-ups	trade-ins
go-betweens	stand-ins
teaspoonfuls	bookshelves
workmen	stockholders

j. The plurals of numerals, alphabet letters, words used as words, and abbreviations composed of initials are formed by using the apostrophe.

Please write your *7's* more legibly.

Your son received three *A's* on his last grade report.

Be sure to dot your *i's.*

Ms. Reed uses too many *and's* in her correspondence.

How many of your graduates earned their *CPA's* last year?

Who will sign the *B.A.'s* granted this year?

k. When referring to two or more individuals by name and title, make plural either the name or the title, but never both.

the *Messrs.* Johnson or the Mr. *Johnsons*

the *Mses.* Smith or the Ms. *Smiths*

8–2. Noun Possessives

a. All nouns not ending with an *s* sound, whether singular or plural, form the possessive by adding *'s.*

office of the *attorney*	attorney's office
toys belonging to the *children*	children's toys
books belonging to *Judy*	Judy's books
lounge for *women*	women's lounge
tax rate of *Illinois*	Illinois's tax rate
(Note: *s* sound is not pronounced in *Illinois.*)	

b. Nouns ending with an *s* sound form the possessive by simply adding an apostrophe unless an additional syllable is pronounced in the possessive form. In the latter case, *'s* is added.

no extra pronounced syllable

the efforts of two *cities*	two cities' efforts
the home belonging to the *Foxes*	the Foxes' home
the pen belonging to Mr. *Simons*	Mr. Simons' pen

extra pronounced syllable

grades of the *class*	the class's grades
the purse belonging to Ms. *Harris*	Ms. Harris's purse

c. In the case of joint ownership, possession is shown only on the last noun. Where individual ownership exists, possession is shown on each noun.

joint ownership

Mary and Alice's apartment has been newly painted.

The Rodriguezes and the Martinsons' mountain cabin closed escrow today.

Mr. Stewart and Ms. Lewis's partnership agreement has been drawn up.

Clark and Clark's handbook is required for this class.

individual ownership

My *mother's and father's* clothes were destroyed in the fire.

Bob's and John's payroll checks were lost.

Mr. Fields' and Ms. Stone's stores are both located on Tampa Avenue.

All *the accountants' and the secretaries'* desks have been moved into the new offices.

d. The possessive form of compound nouns is shown at the end.

investments of my *father-in-law*	*father-in-law's* investments
the report for *stockholders*	the *stockholders'* report
convention of *attorneys-at-law*	*attorneys-at-law's* convention
report of the *personnel manager*	the *personnel manager's* report

e. Use the possessive form before a gerund.

We would appreciate *Lisa's* helping us with the audit.

There is no record of the *witness's* being subpoenaed.

f. Use an apostrophe with the possessives of nouns that refer to time—minutes, hours, days, weeks, months, and years.

singular

peace for a *minute*	a *minute's* peace
work for a *day*	a *day's* work
delay for a *week*	a *week's* delay
notice of a *month*	a *month's* notice

plural

work for four *hours*	four *hours'* work
interest for two *weeks*	two *weeks'* interest
trial for three *months*	three *months'* trial
experience for five *years*	five *years'* experience

g. Do not form possessives for inanimate objects, except time. Instead, use a simple adjective or an *of* phrase.

adjective

The *table* top is scratched. (Not: The table's top is scratched.)

The *typewriter* keys need to be cleaned. (Not: The typewriter's keys need to be cleaned.)

"of" phrase

The door *of the supply cabinet* is jammed. (Not: The supply cabinet's door is jammed.)

The stipulations *of the will* were presented by the attorney. (Not: The will's stipulations were presented by the attorney.)

Pronouns

8–3. Pronoun Case

a. The subjective case pronouns are the following:

I	she	we	who
he	you	they	it

Use a subjective case pronoun (1) for the subject of a sentence, (2) for the complement of a "being" verb, and (3) after the infinitive "to be" when this verb does not have a subject.

subject of a verb

She has applied for the position.

They will arrive at 10 a.m.

complement of a "being" verb

It was *I* who answered the telephone.

The visitors could have been *they*.

infinitive "to be" without a subject

Joalene was thought to be *I*.
It had to be *we* who made the error.

b.   The objective case pronouns are the following:

me	her	us	whom
him	you	them	it

The objective case is used when the pronoun is (1) the object of a verb or preposition, (2) the object of the infinitive "to be" when it has a subject, and (3) the subject or object of any other infinitive.

direct or indirect object of a verb

Mr. Reslaw will meet *her* at the airport tomorrow.

Please place *them* on my desk.

We will mail *him* these copies by Friday.

object of a preposition

This package is *for us.*

Please forward this letter *to her.*

Between you and *me,* I do not believe the plan will be approved.

object of "to be" with a subject

Ms. Stapleton thought *them* to be *us.*

They expected *Mary* to be *me.*

I wanted the *candidate* to be *her.*

subject or object of an infinitive

We thought *them* to be somewhat overconfident.

Our office will not be able to mail *them* until Monday.

We expect *her* to help *us* with the decorations.

c.   The possessive case pronouns are the following:

my	mine
his, her	his, hers
your	yours
our	ours
their	theirs
its	its
	whose

All pronoun possessive case forms are written without apostrophes. They should not be confused with contractions.

possessive pronouns —no apostrophes

Its wrapping had been torn.

Is this sweater *yours?*

The idea was *theirs.*

contractions—apostrophes

It's still raining very heavily here on the West Coast.

Let us know if *you're* going to the convention.

If *there's* a logical reason for the delay, please inform the passengers.

d. Use the possessive case immediately before a gerund.

His leaving the company was quite a surprise.

We would appreciate *your returning* the enclosed card by Friday, March 18.

e. A pronoun after *than* or *as* may be expressed in either the subjective or objective case, depending on whether the pronoun is the subject or object of the following stated or implied verb.

subjective case

Are you as concerned about this matter as *I* am? (Stated verb *am*)

He has been with the company two years longer than *I.* (Implied verb *have*)

objective case

Our editor admires my coauthor more than he admires *me.* (Stated subject and verb *he admires*)

She works for Mr. Reece more hours than *me.* (Implied subject, verb, and preposition *she works for*)

f. Pronouns used in apposition take the same case as those nouns with which they are in apposition.

We, Barbara and *I,* will appear in court tomorrow.

I told Ms. Larsen to submit her expenses to one of our accounting clerks, John or *me.*

g. Pronouns ending in *self* or *selves* emphasize or reflect a noun or pronoun used previously.

emphasize previous noun or pronoun

Mary herself was not pleased with the results of the advertising campaign.

They themselves could not justify their exorbitant budget requests.

reflect a previous noun or pronoun

John addressed the envelope to *himself.*

They agreed to vote *themselves* monthly salary increases of $100.

h. The pronouns *who, whoever; whom, whomever;* and *whose* are used accord-

8

ing to the same rules applied to other personal pronouns. *Who* and *whoever* are used for the subjective case; *whom* and *whomever* are used for the objective case; and *whose* is used for the possessive case.

Isolate the clause in which the pronoun appears; and apply the rules outlined for the subjective, objective, and possessive case pronouns. Be sure to eliminate any extra clause that may appear in the *who, whom,* or *whose* clause.

subjective case—"who" or "whoever"

Mr. Gonzalez is the person *who* was selected for the position.

It was Ms. Graham *who* served as the seventh president of our college.

Who do you think will be appointed to the board? (Omit extra clause *do you think.*)

He is a person *who* I think will be successful in the railroad industry. (Omit extra clause *I think.*)

The city council will ratify the appointment of *whoever* is selected.

objective case—"whom" or "whomever"

He is a person with *whom* we have done business for over twenty-five years.

Whom did Mr. Williams promote to the position of office manager?

The artist *whom* I believe he sponsored moved to New York. (Omit extra clause *I believe.*)

You are a person *whom* I know Ms. Ferraro would be pleased to hire. (Omit extra clause *I know.*)

Whomever you choose for the position, I am sure, will be an excellent employee.

possessive case—"whose"

Whose book is lying here?

We do not know *whose* department will prove to be the most efficient under our new cost-saving plan.

i. Pronouns must agree in gender and number with any nouns they represent.

Everyone please open *his* or *her* book to page 73.

Both *Ms. Greer* and *Mr. Baty* received *their* orders yesterday.

The *puppy* caught *its* tail in the door.

Verbs

8–4. Regular Verbs

Verbs take various forms to designate periods of time. The principal parts of a verb include the present form, the past form, and the past participle.

Regular verbs are all formed in the same way: (1) the present part has the infinitive form without the accompanying *to,* (2) the past tense adds *ed* to the present form, and (3) the past participle uses the past form with at least one verb helper.

infinitive	*present*	*past*	*past participle*
to ask	ask	asked	(have, was) asked
to change	change	changed	(were, had been) changed
to collect	collect	collected	(has, have been) collected

8-5. Irregular Verbs*

Many verbs do not form their parts in the usual manner. These irregular verbs take a variety of forms. A list of parts for commonly used irregular verbs follows:

arise	arose	arisen	lay	laid	laid
become	became	become	lead	led	led
begin	began	begun	leave	left	left
bite	bit	bitten	lend	lent	lent
blow	blew	blown	lie	lay	lain
break	broke	broken	lose	lost	lost
bring	brought	brought	make	made	made
burst	burst	burst	pay	paid	paid
buy	bought	bought	ride	rode	ridden
catch	caught	caught	ring	rang	rung
choose	chose	chosen	rise	rose	risen
come	came	come	run	ran	run
dig	dug	dug	see	saw	seen
do	did	done	set	set	set
draw	drew	drawn	shake	shook	shaken
drink	drank	drunk	shrink	shrank	shrunk
drive	drove	driven	sing	sang	sung
eat	ate	eaten	sink	sank	sunk
fall	fell	fallen	sit	sat	sat
fight	fought	fought	speak	spoke	spoken
fly	flew	flown	spring	sprang	sprung
forget	forgot	forgotten	steal	stole	stolen
forgive	forgave	forgiven	strike	struck	struck
freeze	froze	frozen	swear	swore	sworn
get	got	got	swim	swam	swum
give	gave	given	take	took	taken
go	went	gone	tear	tore	torn
grow	grew	grown	throw	threw	thrown
hang	hung	hung	wear	wore	worn
hide	hid	hidden	write	wrote	written
know	knew	known			

8

---

*Forms of irregular verbs are shown in the dictionary. They are listed after the present form of the verb.

8–6. Use of *Lay* and *Lie*

a. The principal parts of *lay* and *lie* follow:

lay laid laid
lie lay lain

b. Use a form of *lie* when the verb called for is intransitive (does not have a direct object) and a form of *lay* when the verb is transitive (has a direct object). The form is always transitive when the past participle is used with a *being* verb helper.

intransitive

The new shopping center *lies* at the foot of the Flintridge Foothills.

He *lay* in bed for three days with the flu.

transitive

Please *lay* the papers on my desk.

She *laid* the file folders in the "in" tray.

always transitive

These sandbags have *been laid* here because of impending flood damage.

The carpeting for our new building *was laid* yesterday.

8–7. Subject-Verb Agreement

8

a. The verb of a sentence must agree in person and number with the subject. To identify a subject, omit any prepositional phrase that separates the subject and the verb.

The *legs* of the table *were damaged* in transit.

b. Indefinite pronouns such as *each, every, anyone,* and *everyone* take singular verbs.

Each of the books *was* stamped with the company name.

Please give a copy of this report to *anyone* who *asks* for one.

Everyone was pleased with the hotel accommodations.

c. Collective nouns such as *committee, jury, audience, group,* and *council* may take either singular or plural verbs, depending upon the situation in which the verb is used. If the elements of the noun are operating as a unit, use a singular verb; if the elements of the noun are acting separately, use a plural verb.

elements of noun acting as a unit

It is rewarding when an *audience gives* a speaker a standing ovation.

Has the *committee* finished its report?

elements of noun acting separately

The *jury were* arguing violently.

Unfortunately, the *council do* not agree on the purpose of this committee.

d. A relative pronoun clause must agree in gender and number with the noun or pronoun it modifies. Those relative pronoun clauses preceded by such phrases as "one of those doctors," "one of those executives," or "one of those secretaries" agree with the plural noun.

Mary is one of those business *executives* who *travel* considerably in their jobs.

He is one of those *salespersons* who regularly *visit* all their customers.

e. "A number" used as a subject requires a plural verb. "The number" used as a subject requires a singular verb.

"a number" subject

A *number* of our students *have* registered late this semester.

Under the circumstances, a *number* of our customers *are* requesting a full refund.

"the number" subject

The *number* of responses *was* greater than we had expected.

We believe that the *number* of employees selecting the DSE insurance option *has* increased.

f. When *there* precedes the verb, select the singular or plural verb form on the basis of the number of the noun that follows. The same rule applies to those words such as *some, all,* and *part* that indicate portions.

"there" preceding a verb form

There *are* three *people* on the reserve list.

There *appears* to be only one *reason* why we did not receive the contract.

portion preceding a verb form

Some of the *building has* been infested by mice.

Part of your *order has* been shipped.

All the *materials were* shipped to you yesterday.

Only *one-half* of the *packages have* been inspected.

g. Compound subjects joined by *and* require the use of a plural verb. When compound subjects are joined by *or* or *nor* the form of the verb is determined by the second element. If the first element is plural and the second one is singular, switch the two around where possible.

compound joined by "and"

My *son and daughter-in-law receive* monthly issues of the <u>Business Weekly</u>.

Outgoing *letters and packages leave* our office on a regularly scheduled basis.

Mr. Lopez and his two assistants were requested to attend the board meeting.

compound joined by "or" or "nor"

Neither Sharon nor *John was* available for comment to the press.

Either you or *I am* responsible for writing this section of the report.

Ms. Binder or her *assistants are* reviewing the manuscript.

Candy or *flowers are* typically given on this occasion. (Not: Flowers or *candy is* typically given on this occasion.)

Adjectives

8–8. Adjectives Modify Nouns

Adjectives modify nouns. They answer such questions as What kind? How many? Which one?

what kind?

damaged merchandise

green lawns

stylish dresses

how many?

three insurance salespersons

ten years

two dozen pencils

which one?

that chair

those flight attendants

this idea

8–9. Use of the Articles *A* and *An*

Use the article *a* before a word that begins with a consonant sound, a long *u* sound, or an *h* that is pronounced. Use *an* before words that begin with a pronounced vowel sound (except long *u*) or before words that begin with a silent *h*.

use of "a"

a newspaper   a restaurant
a uniform   a union
a history class   a hillside development

use of "an"

an answer   an unusual request
an honest person   an hour

8–10. Adjective Comparison

a.   Adjectives may be used to compare two or more nouns or pronouns. Use the comparative form for comparing two persons or things and the superlative form for comparing three or more.

b.   Regular one-syllable adjectives ending in *e* add *r* for the comparative and *st* for the superlative. Regular one-syllable adjectives ending in consonants add *er* for the comparative and *est* for the superlative.

one-syllable adjectives ending in "e"

He has a *fine* set of golf clubs.

He has a *finer* set of golf clubs than I.

He has the *finest* set of golf clubs I have ever seen.

one-syllable adjectives ending in a consonant

This is a *short* letter.

The first letter is the *shorter* one.

This is the *shortest* letter I have typed today.

c.   Most two-syllable adjectives and all adjectives containing three or more syllables use *more* or *less* and *most* or *least* to form the comparative and superlative. Forms for those two-syllable adjectives that do not follow this pattern are shown in the dictionary. These include *happy, healthy, merry, lovely, pretty*—all ending in *y*.

two- and three-syllable adjectives with "more," "most," "less," or "least"

We purchased a *handsome* wallet yesterday.

This wallet is *more handsome* than the one we purchased yesterday.

This is the *most handsome* wallet in the store.

We purchased an *expensive* wallet yesterday.

This wallet is *less expensive* than the one we purchased yesterday.

This is the *least expensive* wallet in the store.

8

two-syllable adjectives using "er" or "est"

We initiated a *costly* program.

The state's highway program is *costlier* than its conservation program.

Our welfare program is the *costliest* one in the state.

d. Irregular forms for adjective comparison appear in the dictionary. They are listed after the simple forms. A list of commonly used irregular adjectives follows:

simple	*comparative*	*superlative*
good, well	better	best
bad, ill	worse	worst
littie	littler, less	littlest, least
many, much	more	most
far	farther, further	farthest, furthest

e. Use *other* or *else* when comparing one person or object with the other members of the group to which it belongs.

Our Dallas office earns more revenue than any *other* of our branch offices. (Not: "any of our branch offices.")

John is more intelligent than anyone *else* in the class. (Not: "anyone in the class.")

f. Some adjectives cannot be compared in the regular sense because they are absolute. A partial list of such adjectives follows:

finished	perfect	complete
round	dead	straight
unique	full	alive

Absolute adjectives may show comparison by use of the forms "more nearly" or "most nearly."

This water cooler is *full*.

The water cooler in your office is *more nearly full* (not *fuller*) than the one in ours.

The water cooler in the Personnel Office is the *most nearly full* (not *fullest*) one on this floor.

This victim is *dead*.

This victim is *more nearly dead* (not *deader*) than the other one.

This victim is the *most nearly dead* (not *deadest*) one on the hospital floor.

8–11. Independent Adjectives

When two or more adjectives appearing before a noun independently modify the noun, separate these adjectives with commas.

His *direct, practical* approach to problems created high respect among his staff.

We returned that *boring, poorly written* manuscript to its author.

She handled the problem in a *sure, calm, decisive* manner.

8–12. Adjectives With Linking Verbs

Use adjectives after linking verbs. Common linking verbs include *feel, look, smell, sound,* and *taste.*

I *feel bad* that you were not elected.

This cake *tastes delicious.*

After the fire the adjoining rooms *smelled terrible.*

8–13. Compound Adjectives

When one or more words appearing before a noun function as a single adjective, place hyphens between the words.

Your *up-to-date* files have been very helpful in compiling this data.

Upon reading your *well-written* report, the committee members agreed to establish a new community center.

Adverbs

8–14. Function and Form of Adverbs

8

Adverbs modify verbs, adjectives, or other adverbs. They answer such questions as When? Where? Why? How? To what degree?

a. Most adverbs end in *ly.*

accidentally	daily	finally
carefully	definitely	steadily
cautiously	diligently	usually

b. Some adverbs (mostly ones containing one syllable) may either end in *ly* or take the adjective form of the word.*

Please drive *slowly* (or *slow*) on this icy road.

Your order will be processed as *quickly* (or *quick*) as possible.

You may call *directly* (or *direct*) to Chicago on this line.

---

*Both forms are shown in the dictionary for those adverbs that may end in *ly* or take the adjective form.

c. Other adverbs do not take an *ly* form. Such adverbs include the following:

again	not	there
almost	now	very
never	soon	well

8–15. Adverb Comparison

a. One-syllable adverbs and some two-syllable adverbs are compared by adding *er* or *est.* For comparisons between two items, use *er;* for comparisons among more than two items, use *est.**

comparisons of two

You live *closer* to the library than I.

My assistant left *earlier* than I.

comparisons of more than two

Of all the students in the study group, you live *closest* to the library.

Of all the conference members, Ms. Jansen left *earliest* for the airport.

b. Most adverbs containing two syllables and all adverbs containing more than two syllables form the comparison by adding *more* or *most* to the positive form. Use *more* in comparing two items and *most* in comparing more than two items.

comparisons of two

This brand of soap is *more widely* used on the East Coast than in the South.

This conveyor belt travels *more slowly* than the one next to it.

Please pack these items *more carefully* than you have done in the past.

comparisons of more than two

This brand of soap is the *most widely* used one in the country.

Denver has been mentioned *most often* as the likely site for our next convention.

This conference is the *most unusually* conducted one I have ever attended.

8–16. Adverbs vs. Adjectives

Use an adverb after a verb that shows action; use an adjective, however, after a nonaction (or linking) verb.

action verb

The pedestrian *crossed* the street *cautiously.*

---

*Two-syllable adverbs that show comparison by adding *er* or *est* are considered irregular. Therefore, they are shown in the dictionary following the simple form.

Our senator *opposed bitterly* the controversial measure.

This food *was prepared hastily.*

Our bowling team *was beaten badly.*

nonaction or linking verb

This room *smells terrible.*

His coffee *tastes bitter.*

I *feel bad* about Mr. Johnson's predicament.

The Sunday evening banquet *was delicious.*

8–17. Double Negatives

Use only one negative or limiting adverb to express a single idea.

I *can* (not *can't*) *scarcely* believe that our president would make such a foolish statement.

We *were* (not *weren't*) *hardly* in the office when Ms. Murch gave us the disappointing news.

He *had* (not *hadn't*) *barely* finished the report in time for the board meeting.

Do *not* release this information to *anybody* (not *nobody*).

Prepositions

8

8–18. In, Between, or Among?

When the preposition has a single object, use *in.* For two separate objects, use *between;* for three or more objects, use *among.*

"in"

There are several discrepancies *in* the auditor's report.

The prosecution noted several discrepancies *in* the witness's testimony.

"between"

Between you and me, I believe our company stock will split within the next several months.

There were several discrepancies *between* the two witnesses' reports.

"among"

Please distribute these supplies *among* the various branch offices.

Among themselves the Board of Directors consented previously to withdraw that motion.

8–19. Prepositions Used With Certain Words

Certain words require certain prepositions, depending upon the meaning to be conveyed. A list of commonly used combinations follows:

Agree *on* or *upon* (reach an understanding)
Agree *to* (undertake an action)
Agree *with* (a person or his or her idea)

Angry *about* (a situation or condition)
Angry *with* (a person or a group of persons)

Buy *from* (not *off*)

Compare *with* (measure)
Compare *to* (show resemblance)

Comply or compliance *with* (not *to*)

Conform *to* (bring in harmony with—transitive verb)
Conform *with* (be in harmony with—intransitive verb)

Convenient *to* (a person or an object)
Convenient *for* (a purpose)

Correspond *with* (by writing)
Correspond *to* (a thing)

Differ *from* (a person or thing)
Differ *from, with,* or *about* (an idea or opinion)
Different *from* (not *than*)

Identical *with* (not *to*)

Off (not off *of*)

Opposite (not opposite *to* or *of*)

Plan *to* (not *on*)

Retroactive *to* (not *from*)

8–20. Prepositional Phrases

In determining subject-verb agreement, generally omit any prepositional phrases that separate the subject and the verb.

One of your brothers *is* waiting in your office.

A large *quantity* of goods *has* been ordered for the sale.

Last Monday our *supply* of paper goods and kitchen utensils *was* destroyed.

Conjunctions

8–21. Conjunctions Used in Pairs

a. Use *either . . . or* for positive statements; use *neither . . . nor* for negative statements.

positive statements, "either . . . or"

Either Ms. Saunders *or* Mr. Ramirez will inspect the property.

You may specify *either* black *or* brown on your order.

negative statements, "neither . . . nor"

Neither a Toyota *nor* a Datsun is available for rental this week.

I could not believe that *neither* Larry *nor* Debbie would accept the assignment.

b. Use the same grammatical construction after each part of the conjunctive pair *not only . . . but also.*

Our company manufactures *not only* furniture *but also* major appliances. (Not: Our company *not only* manufactures furniture *but also* major appliances.)

Our company *not only* manufactures and services major appliances *but also* services small appliances.

c. In comparisons, use *as . . . as* for positive ideas and *so . . . as* for negative ideas.

positive ideas, "as . . . as"

Our Model 874 radio has become *as* popular *as* our Model 923.

I believe that her understudy is *as* talented *as* Mr. Saito.

negative ideas, "so . . . as"

Our Model 874 radio is not *so* popular *as* our Model 923.

Avocados are not *so* expensive *as* they were last year.

8–22. As vs. Like

As is a conjunction and is used when the following construction is a clause (contains a subject and a verb). *Like* is a preposition and is used when the following construction is a prepositional object (a phrase ending with a noun or pronoun).

"as" with a clause

They did not package the order *as* (not *like*) *he expected they would.*

155

As (not *like*) *you indicated in your letter,* we cannot expect to make a profit during our first year of operations.

"like" with a prepositional phrase

We need more qualified agents *like you.*

Please order another typewriter *like the one* you have in your office.

8

9
address format and forms of address

9

Address Format and Forms of Address Solution Finder

9

General Format

9–1. General Address Format

a. Use combinations of the following to address general business correspondence: full name with appropriate title, company name, street address, city, state, and zip code. Use the same format for both the inside address and the envelope, unless the company uses the envelope format described in 10–26.

addressed to individual

Ms. Elizabeth Bennett
2879 Balboa Boulevard, Apt. 2
San Clemente, California 92672

Dear Ms. Bennett:

addressed to individual within company

Mr. Jay V. Berger, Manager
Policy Issue Department
General Insurance Company of America
341 Prospect Avenue
Hartford, Connecticut 06105

Dear Mr. Berger:

addressed to company

F. M. Tarbell Company
2740 Troy Avenue, S.W.
Indianapolis, Indiana 46241

Attention: Mr. William F. Schlossinger, Manager, Personnel Department

Gentlemen:

b. An address may have a maximum of six lines and a minimum of two lines.

minimum two-line address

Phillips Foods, Inc.
Morristown, NJ 07960

maximum six-line address

Miss Stephanie R. Whitaker
Chief Operations Manager
Quality Control Department
Neware Aluminum Accessories
3618 Chelwood Boulevard, N.E.
Albuquerque, NM 87111

Names and Titles

9–2. Courtesy Titles

a. Abbreviate the courtesy titles *Mr., Ms.,* and *Mrs.* when they are used with the names of individuals. Spell out, however, the title *Miss.*

Mr. Stanley Hutchinson

Ms. Nina Lopez

Mrs. Charlene Carnachan

Miss Frances Cates

b. When the name of an individual does not signify whether the person is a man or a woman, omit the courtesy title or use the title *Mr.* When addressing a woman, use the courtesy title *Ms.* unless *Miss* or *Mrs.* is specified by the addressee.

Chris Kenworth

Mr. Lynn V. Stauber

Ms. Elizabeth Rankin

c. The title *Master* is used for addressing young boys (boys too young to be called *Mister*).

Master William J. Clark

d. The abbreviated courtesy title *Esq.* is sometimes used after the surname. In such cases, no courtesy title precedes the name.

Murray T. Silverstein, *Esq.*

9–3. Professional Titles

9

a. Write out and capitalize all professional titles, except *Dr.* and long professional titles, when they precede the names of individuals. *Professor, Dean, The Reverend, Governor, Colonel,* and *The Honorable* are examples of titles that are capitalized and written in full.

"Doctor" abbreviated

Dr. Allen Kupsh

professional title written out

Professor Marly Bergerud

long professional title abbreviated

Lt.-Col. Ret. Maurice P. Wiener

b. In addressing business correspondence or completing signature lines, capitalize and write out professional titles that follow an individual's name.

single-line address format

Mr. Ray Johnson, *Dean*

two-line address format

Ms. Jane S. Kenyon
Plant Superintendent

single-line signature format

Ruth Johnson, *Dean*

two-line signature format

John S. Kenyon
Plant Superintendent

c. Capitalize professional titles not appearing in address format or signature lines only when they precede an individual's name. Do not capitalize titles following an individual's name, except in the case of high-ranking government officials (President of the United States, Vice-President of the United States, Cabinet members, Congressional senators, and governors).

title preceding name

President Robert I. Place will deliver the main address.

title following name

Robert I. Place, *president* of A & I Enterprises, will deliver the main address.

title of high-ranking government official

The Honorable John Linn, *Senator* from Pennsylvania, has agreed to deliver the main address.

d. Only one professional courtesy title with the same meaning should appear with a single name. Use *Dr.* or *M.D.* but not both titles with the same name.

titles with the same meaning

Dr. James V. Glaser
James V. Glaser, *M.D.*

titles with different meanings

Dr. Barbara Simi, *Professor*

e. Do not capitalize professional titles that substitute for individuals' names, except in the case of high-ranking government officials.

title substituted for name

The *general* scheduled a staff meeting for Thursday afternoon.

9

title of high-ranking government official

Did the *Governor* appear for the press conference?

9–4. Company Names

Spell out company names in full, unless the company itself uses abbreviations in its official name. *Inc.* and *Ltd.* usually appear in abbreviated form.

company name written in full

Pacific Mutual Life Insurance Company

company name containing abbreviation

Consolidated Factors, *Ltd.*

Places

9–5. Buildings and Units

Capitalize the names of buildings and units therein.

Capitol Building, Office 243F

Medical Arts Center, Suite 680–681

Greenwich Apartments, Unit 3

9–6. Street Addresses

a. Use figures to express house numbers. Only the house number *one* is written in word form.

house number one

One Lakeview Terrace

house number in figures

8 Burbank Lane

b. Spell out compass directions that appear within a street address. Abbreviate compass points following the street address.

compass point within street address

1864 *East* 37 Street

compass point following street address

180 Central Avenue, *S.W.*

c. Numbered street names *ten* and below are written in words (using ordinal numbers—first, second, third, etc.). Numbered street names above *ten*, however, are written in figures. Use cardinal numbers (1, 2, 3, etc.) when a compass point appears between the house and street numbers; use ordinal numbers (1st, 2d, 3d, etc.) when no such compass point is present.

numbered street name ten or below

1183 *Fifth* Avenue

numbered street name above ten—with compass point

980 North *81* Street

numbered street name above ten—without compass point

2036 *48th* Street

d. Spell out where possible street designations such as *Boulevard, Avenue, Street, Place,* and *Lane.* Abbreviate designation *Boulevard (Blvd.)* only with long addresses.

street name spelled out

18394 Lankershim *Boulevard*

street name abbreviated

19263 North Coldwater Canyon *Blvd.*

e. Spell out where possible mailing designations such as *Rural Route* or *Post Office Box* that are used in the place of street addresses. Abbreviate the mailing designation only with long addresses.

postal designation spelled out

Post Office Box 107

postal designation abbreviated

P. O. Box 269, Terminal Annex

f. Apartment, building, and unit numbers are expressed in figures and are typed on the same line as the street address. The terms *Apartment* and *Building* may be abbreviated when they are included with a street address.

unit number

6176 Arroyo Road, *Unit* 2

apartment number

3964 West 81 Street, *Apt.* 3

no specific designation

16932 Wilshire Boulevard, *C-110*

9

9–7. City, State, and Zip Code

a. Spell out in full the names of cities.

Saint Louis	New York
Fort Worth	Los Angeles

b. Use the two-letter post office designation for state names or spell out in full the state name. Select either mode based upon (1) the degree of formality of the correspondence or (2) the one that provides better balance for setting up the entire address. Should both be equally suitable, use the two-letter postal designation. Use the same form for both the inside address and the envelope, unless the company chooses to use the U.S. Post Office recommendations for addressing envelopes described in 10–26.

state two-letter zip code designation

Ms. Jessica Moore
108 Academy Avenue
Boston, MA 02188

state name written in full

Mr. William R. Stephenson
257 American Legion Highway
Boston, Massachusetts 02131

c. Zip codes are typed a single space after the state.

Atlanta, Georgia 30331

Atlanta, GA 30331

9 Forms of Address

9–8. Forms of Address

The following list shows the proper form of address, salutation, and complimentary close for specific addressees. When the addressee is a woman, substitute one of the following for the salutation shown:

Madam for *Mr.* before formal terms such as *President, Vice-President, Chairman, Secretary, Ambassador,* and *Minister.*

Ms., Miss, or *Mrs.* for *Mr.* before the name of a member of the House of Representatives, a senator-elect, a representative-elect, or a lesser government official.

Addressee	Address on Letter and Envelope	Salutation and Complimentary Close
The President	The President The White House Washington, DC 20500	Dear Mr. President: Respectfully,
Wife of the President	Mrs. (full name) The White House Washington, DC 20500	Dear Mrs. (surname): Sincerely,
Assistant to the President	Honorable (full name) Assistant to the President The White House Washington, DC 20500	Dear Mr. (surname): Sincerely,
The Vice-President	The Vice-President United States Senate Washington, DC 20510 or The Honorable (full name) Vice-President of the United States Washington, DC 20501	Dear Mr. Vice-President: Sincerely,

The Chief Justice	The Chief Justice of the
	  United States
	The Supreme Court of the
	  United States
	Washington, DC 20543
		Dear Mr. Chief Justice:
		Sincerely,

Associate Justice	Mr. Justice (surname) The Supreme Court of the United States Washington, DC 20543	Dear Mr. Justice: Sincerely,
United States Senator	Honorable (full name) United States Senate Washington, DC 20510 or Honorable (full name) United States Senator (local address) 00000	Dear Senator (surname): Sincerely,
United States Representative	Honorable (full name) House of Representatives Washington, DC 20515 or Honorable (full name) Member, United States House of Representatives (local address) 00000	Dear Mr. (surname): Sincerely,

9

Address Format and Forms of Address

Addressee	Address on Letter and Envelope	Salutation and Complimentary Close
Cabinet Members	Honorable (full name) Secretary of (name of department) Washington, DC 00000	Dear Mr. Secretary: Sincerely,
	or	
	Honorable (full name) Postmaster General Washington, DC 20260	Dear Mr. Postmaster General: Sincerely,
	or	
	Honorable (full name) Attorney General Washington, DC 20530	Dear Mr. Attorney General: Sincerely,
Deputy Secretaries, Assistants, or Under Secretaries	Honorable (full name) Deputy Secretary of (name of department) Washington, DC 00000	Dear Mr. (surname): Sincerely,
	or	
	Honorable (full name) Assistant Secretary of (name of department) Washington, DC 00000	
	or	
	Honorable (full name) Under Secretary of (name of department) Washington, DC 00000	
Head of Independent Offices and Agencies	Honorable (full name) Comptroller General of the United States General Accounting Office Washington, DC 20548	Dear Mr. (surname): Sincerely,
	or	
	Honorable (full name) Chairman, (name of commission) Washington, DC 00000	Dear Mr. Chairman: Sincerely,
	or	
	Honorable (full name) Director, Bureau of the Budget Washington, DC 20503	Dear Mr. (surname): Sincerely,
American Ambassador	Honorable (full name) American Ambassador (City), (Country)	Sir: (formal) Dear Mr. Ambassador (informal) Very truly yours, (formal) Sincerely, (informal)

Addressee	Address on Letter and Envelope	Salutation and Complimentary Close
American Consul General or American Consul	(Full name) American Consul General (or American Consul) (City), (Country)	Dear Mr. (surname): Sincerely,
Foreign Ambassador in the United States	His Excellency (full name) Ambassador of (country) (local address) 00000	Excellency: (formal) Dear Mr. Ambassador: (informal) Very truly yours, (formal) Sincerely, (informal)
Governor of State	Honorable (full name) Governor of (name of state) (City), (State) 00000	Dear Governor (surname): Sincerely,
Lieutenant Governor	Honorable (full name) Lieutenant Governor of (name of state) (City), (State) 00000	Dear Mr. (surname): Sincerely,
State Senator	Honorable (full name) (name of state) Senate (City), (State) 00000	Dear Mr. (surname): Sincerely,
State Representative, Assemblyman, or Delegate	Honorable (full name) (name of state) House of Representatives (or Assembly or House of Delegates) (City), (State) 00000	Dear Mr. (surname): Sincerely,
Mayor	Honorable (full name) Mayor of (name of city) (City), (State) 00000	Dear Mr. (surname): Sincerely,
President of a Board of Commissioners	Honorable (full name) President, Board of Commissioners of (name of city) (City), (State) 00000	Dear Mr. (surname): Sincerely,
Judge	Honorable (full name) (name of court) (local address) 00000	Dear Judge (surname): Sincerely,
Protestant Clergy	The Right Reverend (full name) Bishop of (name) (local address) 00000	Right Reverend Sir: (formal) Dear Bishop (surname): (informal) Sincerely,
	or	
	The Very Reverend (full name) Dean of (name of church) (local address) 00000	Very Reverend Sir: (formal) Dear Dean (surname): (informal) Sincerely,

9

Addressee	Address on Letter and Envelope	Salutation and Complimentary Close
	or	
	The Reverend (full name) Bishop of (name) (local address) 00000	Reverend Sir: (formal) Dear Bishop (surname): (informal) Sincerely,
	or	
	The Reverend (full name) (Title), (name of church) (local address) 00000	Dear Reverend (surname): Dear Mr. (surname): Sincerely,
Catholic Clergy	His Eminence (given name) Cardinal (surname) Archbishop of (diocese) (local address) 00000	Your Eminence: (formal) Dear Cardinal (surname): (informal) Sincerely,
	or	
	The Most Reverend (full name) Archbishop of (diocese) (local address) 00000	Your Excellency: (formal) Dear Archbishop (surname): (informal) Sincerely,
	or	
	The Most Reverend (full name) Bishop of (city) (local address) 00000	Your Excellency: (formal) Dear Bishop (surname): (informal) Sincerely,
	or	
	The Right Reverend Monsignor (full name) (local address) 00000	Right Reverend Monsignor: (formal) Dear Monsignor (surname): (informal) Sincerely,
	or	
	The Very Reverend Monsignor (full name) (local address) 00000	Very Reverend Monsignor: (formal) Dear Monsignor (surname): (informal) Sincerely,
	or	
	The Reverend (full name) (add initials of order, if any) (local address) 00000	Reverend Sir: (formal) Dear Father (surname): (informal) Sincerely,
	or	
	Mother (full name) (initials of order, if used) Superior (name of convent) (local address) 00000	Dear Mother (full name): Sincerely,

9

Addressee	Address on Letter and Envelope	Salutation and Complimentary Close
	or	
	Sister (full name) (initials of order, if used) (name of convent) (local address) 00000	Dear Sister (full name): Sincerely,
Jewish Clergy	Rabbi (full name) (local address) 00000	Dear Rabbi (surname): Sincerely,
Chaplains	Chaplain (full name) (rank, service designation) (post office address of organization and station) (local address) 00000	Dear Chaplain (surname): Sincerely,
President of a College or University (Doctor)	Dr. (full name) President, (name of institution) (local address) 00000	Dear Dr. (surname): Sincerely,
Dean of a School	Dean (full name) School of (name) (name of institution) (local address) 00000	Dear Dean (surname): Sincerely,
Professor	Professor (full name) Department of (name) (name of institution) (local address) 00000	Dear Professor (surname): Sincerely,
Physician	(full name), M.D. (local address) 00000	Dear Dr. (surname): Sincerely,
Lawyer	Mr. (full name) Attorney at Law (local address) 00000	Dear Mr. (surname): Sincerely,
Widow	Mrs. (husband's first name, last name) (local address) 00000	Dear Mrs. (surname): Sincerely,
	or	
	Mrs. (wife's first name, last name)* (local address) 00000	Dear Mrs. (surname): Sincerely,

*This form is also used for a woman who is separated or divorced from her husband or for a married woman who has so signed.

Address Format and Forms of Address

Addressee	Address on Letter and Envelope	Salutation and Complimentary Close
	or	
	Ms. (wife's first name, last name) (local address) 00000	Dear Ms. (surname): Sincerely,
Two or More Men	Mr. (full name) and Mr. (full name) (local address) 00000	Dear Mr. (surname) and Mr. (surname): Dear Messrs. (surname) and (surname): Gentlemen: Sincerely,
Two or More Women	Mrs. (full name) and Mrs. (full name) (local address) 00000 or	Dear Mrs. (surname) and Mrs. (surname): Dear Mesdames (surname) and (surname): Mesdames: Sincerely,
	Miss (full name) and Mrs. (full name) (local address) 00000 or	Dear Miss (surname) and Mrs. (surname): Sincerely,
	Ms. (full name) and Ms. (full name) (local address) 00000	Dear Ms. (surname) and Ms. (surname): Sincerely,
One Woman and One Man	Ms. (full name) and Mr. (full name) (local address) 00000	Dear Ms. (surname) and Mr. (surname): Sincerely,
Married Couple	Mr. and Mrs. (husband's full name) (local address) 00000	Dear Mr. and Mrs. (surname): Sincerely,
Professional Married Couple	(title) (full name of husband) (title) (full name of wife) (local address) 00000	Dear (title) and (title) (surname): Dear (plural of title and surname if both husband and wife have same title): Sincerely,
Service Personnel	(full grade, name, and abbreviation of service designation) (Retired is added if applicable) (title and organization) (local address) 00000	Dear (grade) (surname): Sincerely,

10

business letters and memorandums

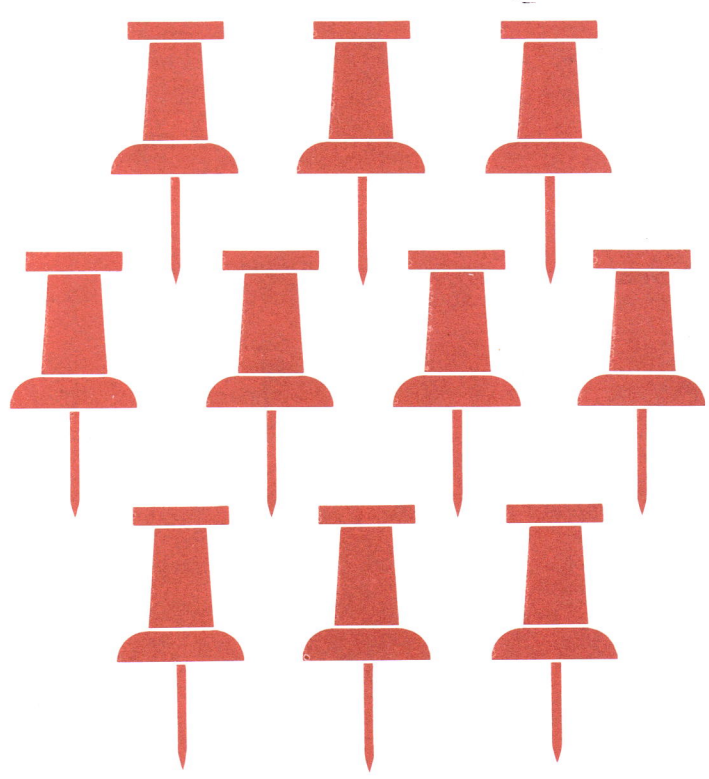

10

Business Letters and Memorandums Solution Finder

10

Letter Styles

10–1. Full Block

The full block letter style is the most efficient letter style because all parts and all lines begin at the left margin.

full block letter

Gibraltar Insurance Company of America

916 New Britain Avenue
Hartford, Connecticut 06106
Telephone: (203) 743-1200

June 16, 1979

Lynch & Marten Insurance Agency
16320 San Fernando Mission Boulevard
Sepulveda, California 91343

Gentlemen

SUBJECT: CLAIM NO. AT 6509, INSURED THOMAS A. GLASCO

The claim of your client, Mr. Thomas A. Glasco, for $300 to
replace the golf clubs that were stolen from him in Las Vegas
is covered under his homeowner's policy, No. 19362084.

To process Mr. Glasco's claim, we must have a copy of the
police report filed at the time of the theft. Please contact
the police agency handling the theft report and have them
forward us a copy addressed to my attention.

As soon as we receive the necessary information, Mr. Glasco's
check will be sent to your office.

Sincerely yours

GIBRALTAR INSURANCE COMPANY OF AMERICA

Mariam R. Marsh, Claims Adjuster

fd

cc: Mr. Thomas A. Glasco

10

10–2. Modified Block

a. The modified block letter style with blocked paragraphs is the most popular letter style used in business. All lines except the return address (if used), the date, and the closing lines begin at the left margin.

modified block letter with blocked paragraphs

Dickens Crystal, Inc.

1640 Grand Boulevard
Schenectady, New York 12309
Telephone: (518) 872-3100

April 17, 1980

House of Imports
5700 Oxford Avenue
Philadelphia, PA 19149

Attention Ms. Jody Stevens, Buyer

Gentlemen:

Our complete line of Dickens Crystal is illustrated in the enclosed
catalog. As you will note from the full-page color illustrations, its
simple design and exquisite workmanship have made Dickens crystal one
of the most popular lines in the country.

We appreciate your interest in our products and would be pleased to have
the House of Imports carry them. I am sure you would find these fast-
selling gift items a profitable addition to your inventory.

A complete list of prices and the terms of sale are included in the back
pages of the catalog. You will also note that we serve you by providing
a breakage credit up to 5 percent of purchases on merchandise displayed
in your store. Just return any broken pieces, and we will replace the
merchandise.

We hope that we can add your name to the many retailers throughout the
country who represent Dickens crystal. Should you wish to open an
account with us, please return the enclosed credit application forms.
If you wish to place a c.o.d. order, we can deliver the merchandise
within ten days of the receipt of your order.

Let Dickens start earning for you today.

Sincerely,

Edward T. Cowan
Vice-President, Marketing

ma
Enclosures

---

b. The modified block letter style with indented paragraphs is also used frequently. All lines except the first line of each paragraph, the return address (if used), the date, and the closing lines begin at the left margin.

modified block letter with indented paragraphs

Lawndale Pharmaceutical Company

5170 Medina Road
Akron, Ohio 44321
Telephone: (216) 382-4955

November 3, 1979

Mr. Daryl M. Huggins
Personnel Manager
Rochester Laboratories
8100 East North Loop
Houston, TX 77029

Dear Mr. Huggins:

Orville T. White, one of your former salespeople, has applied for a sales position with our company and has given your name as reference. May we have your frank appraisal of his abilities as a salesperson of pharmaceutical supplies?

Naturally, any information you give us about Mr. White's potential for success in our organization will be kept strictly confidential.

We would appreciate receiving your appraisal of Mr. White within the next few days, as we are anxious to fill a sales opening on our staff. And, of course, if ever in the future we can provide you information about one of your applicants, we would be happy to do so.

Sincerely yours,

John T. Morrison
Director of Personnel

mb

10

10–3. Personal Business

The personal business letter style is used for personal business correspondence. The inside address is placed after the closing lines in this informal format. The salutation may be followed by a comma instead of a colon. Paragraphs are either indented or blocked. The typed signature line is optional. Reference initials, enclosure notations, and carbon copy notations are usually omitted on the original, but these parts may be typed below the inside address on the file copy or on the copies for distribution. Leave a double space after the inside address and single-space the information to be included.

personal business letter

United Bank of Iowa

Park Fair Shopping Center
Des Moines, Iowa 50313
Telephone: (515) 273-9600

January 23, 1979

Dear Jim,

Congratulations on your appointment as president of Bayview Savings and Loan Association and executive vice-president of the parent holding company, Consolidated Financial Corporation.

You are certainly deserving of this promotion because you have contributed immeasurably to the rapid growth and development of Bayview and Consolidated. I know, too, that under your leadership both organizations will continue to move forward in the savings and loan industry.

Sincerely,

John S. Moore

Mr. James T. Montague, President
Bayview Savings and Loan Association
5800 West Camelback Road
Phoenix, Arizona 85033

10

10–4. Simplified

The simplified letter style was introduced by the Administrative Management Society. All parts of the letter begin at the left margin. In this style a subject line typed in all capital letters replaces the salutation. Two blank lines are left before and after the subject line. No complimentary close is used in the simplified letter style. Instead, the signature line is typed on the fifth line below the last line of the message. Use all capital letters and a single line for the signature line.

simplified letter

John Hancock Mutual Life Insurance Company

200 Berkeley Street
Boston, Massachusetts 02117

June 7, 1979

Mr. Stanley R. Chow
Acme Insurance Agency
200 East Fulton Street
Grand Rapids, MI 49502

POLICY NO. J783294, INSURED JOHN R. WILLIAMS

We have completed our investigation of the accident claim submitted by your
agency on behalf of John R. Williams.

According to our claims adjuster, Mr. Williams was injured while in the
employ of the Deluxe Manufacturing Company. His injuries were incurred in
an industrial accident on March 3 and are totally job related. Consequently,
the expenses of this accident are covered by Workers' Compensation. Only
those expenses beyond the amount allowed by Workers' Compensation are covered
by our company.

Please submit a complete listing of Mr. Williams' expenses in regard to this
accident. As soon as we receive verification from the Workers' Compensation
Board on the amount allowable in Mr. Williams' case, we will process the
proper claim forms, if applicable.

If you have any questions or need any additional information, please let us
know.

B. WILLIAM COLTON, C.L.U., SENIOR VICE PRESIDENT

mrd

10

Placement of Major Letter Parts

10–5. Return Address

a. No return address is needed for business letters typed on paper containing a complete company letterhead. When plain bond paper or letterhead paper without a mailing address is used, a return address must be included.

b. On plain paper begin the return address so that the last line is 2 inches from the top of the paper. The following table may be used to determine return address placement.

Return Address Placement

Number of Lines in Address	Typing Line for First Line of Address
2	11
3	10
4	9
5	8

In the full block and simplified letter styles, all lines begin at the left margin. In the modified block or personal business styles, the return address may (1) begin at the center of the page, (2) begin five spaces to the left of the page center, (3) have the longest line back-spaced from the right margin to determine the placement, or (4) have each line centered.

return address in full block or simplified letter style without letterhead

10

178

return address in modified block or personal business letter style without letterhead

```
                                                                    1
                                                                    2
                                                                    3
                                                                    4
                                                                    5
                                                                    6
                                                                    7
                                                                    8
                                                                    9
                                                                   10
                          2034 Mason Street                        11
                          Macon, Georgia 31204                     12
```

c. On letterhead paper without a mailing address, begin the return address a double space below the last line in the letterhead or end it 2 inches below the top edge of the paper. Select the procedure that places the return address in the lower position.

return address begun a double space below letterhead—full block or simplified letter

```
                                                                    1
                                                                    2
          Committee for the Reelection of the Governor             3
                                                                    4
                   A Nonprofit Organization                        5
                                                                    6
     Endorsed by:                                                  7
     _____   _____   _____   _____         8
                                                                    9
     _____   _____   _____   _____        10
                                                                   11
     _____   _____   _____   _____        12
                                                                   13
     9978 Access Road                                             14
     Minneapolis, MN 55431                                        15
```

return address ending 2 inches from top edge of paper—modified block or personal business letter

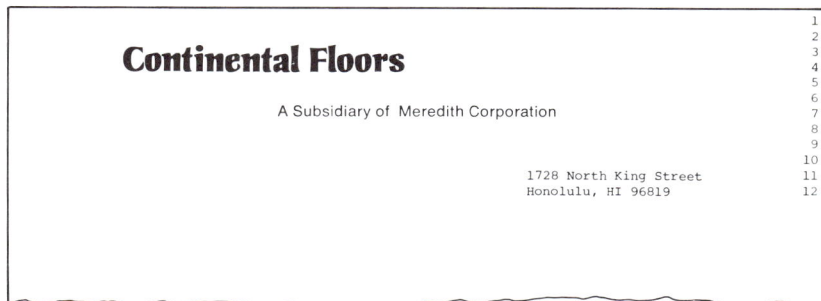

179

10–6. Date

a. On letterhead paper with a mailing address, type the date a double space below the last line in the letterhead or with a 2-inch margin from the top edge of the paper (line 13). Select the procedure that places the date in the lower position.

In full block or simplified letters, type the date at the left margin. In modified block and personal business letters, the date may be centered, begun at the center of the paper, or back-spaced from the right margin.

date typed a double space below letterhead—full block letter

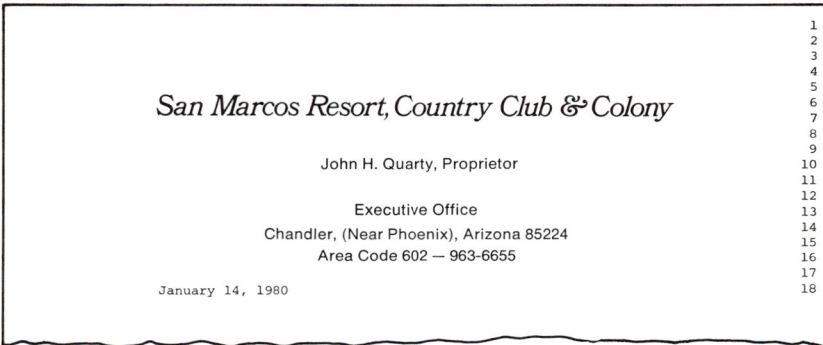

```
                                                                          1
                                                                          2
                                                                          3
                                                                          4
                                                                          5
        San Marcos Resort, Country Club & Colony                          6
                                                                          7
                                                                          8
                                                                          9
                 John H. Quarty, Proprietor                              10
                                                                         11
                                                                         12
                    Executive Office                                     13
            Chandler, (Near Phoenix), Arizona 85224                      14
                 Area Code 602 — 963-6655                                15
                                                                         16
                                                                         17
        January 14, 1980                                                 18
```

date typed 2 inches below top edge of paper—modified block or personal business letter

```
                                                                          1
                                                                          2
            Los Angeles Pierce College                                    3
                                                                          4
                                                                          5
                                                                          6
                  6201 Winnetka Avenue                                    7
              Woodland Hills, California 91364                             8
                 Telephone: (213) 347-0551                                9
                                                                         10
                                                                         11
                                                                         12
                  May 8, 1979                                            13
```

b. In letters requiring return addresses, type the date on the line directly below the last line of the return address.

10

date with return address

10–7. Personal and Mailing Notations

a. Personal notations such as *Personal* and *Confidential* are typed in all capital letters either (1) a double space below and even with the date or (2) a double space above the inside address.

even with date

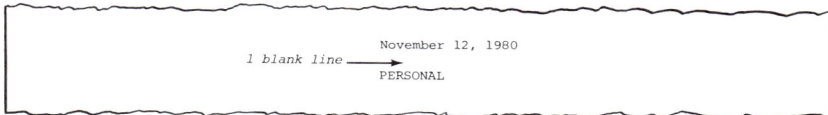

double space above inside address

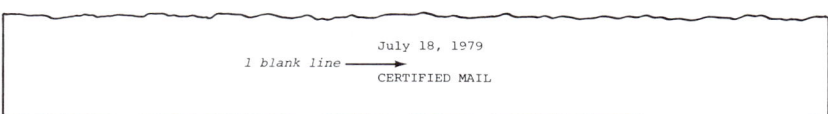

b. Mailing notations such as *Special Delivery, Registered Mail,* and *Certified Mail* are typed in all capital letters (1) a double space below and even with the date, (2) a double space above the inside address, or (3) a single or double space below the reference initials or enclosure notation, whichever appears last.

10

even with date

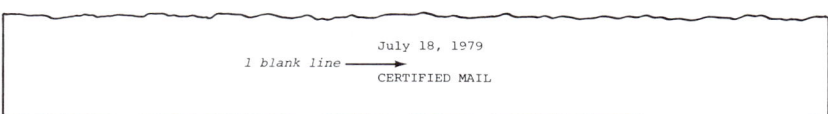

double space above inside address

```
SPECIAL DELIVERY
          ◄——————1 blank line
Dr. Edward L. Adams
933 Westminster Street
Providence, RI 02904
```

after reference initials or enclosure notation

```
dls
Enclosures 3
REGISTERED MAIL
cc:  Mr. Roland B. Sink
```

c.   If a personal notation and a mailing notation appear in the same letter, place the personal notation a triple space above the inside address and the mailing notation on the line directly below. Both notations are typed in all capital letters. Leave at least two blank lines between the date and the personal notation.

personal and mailing notation in same letter

```
February 11, 1980
                    ◄——————at least 2 blank lines
CONFIDENTIAL
SPECIAL DELIVERY
               ◄——————1 blank line
Mr. Frank D. Parsons
Vice-President, Sales
Western Foundry, Inc.
3210 West Polk Street
Chicago, IL 60612
```

10–8.   Inside Address

10

a.   The inside address contains some or all of the following: courtesy title, name, professional title, company name, street or mailing address, city, state, and zip code. Single-space and begin at the left margin those parts necessary to direct the letter to the addressee.

arrangement of an inside address

Miss Phyllis I. Prescott
Manager, Accounting Department
Eastern Savings and Loan Association
6750 East Independence Boulevard
Charlotte, North Carolina 28212

b.   Abbreviate only the courtesy titles *Mr., Mrs., Ms.,* and *Dr.* Spell out all street designations such as *Street, Avenue,* and *Boulevard*, except in exceptionally long street addresses. Spell out the state name or use the two-letter post office designation, whichever achieves balance with the remaining lines. Each inside address should contain a minimum of two lines and a maximum of six lines.

two-line inside address

Holiday Inn
Cedar Rapids, IA 52406

six-line inside address

Mr. M. J. Fujimoto
Airline Training Specialist
Division of Personnel Instruction
Trans Continental Airlines
12700 East Funston Street
Wichita, Kansas 67207

c. In the modified, full block, and simplified letter styles, the inside address usually follows the date. The number of blank lines between the date and the inside address is determined by the length of the letter. Generally, the following table may be used for 8 1/2-by-11-inch paper to determine (1) the number of lines between the date and the inside address and (2) the margins to be used for typing the letter.

Inside Address Placement

Approximate Number of Words in Body of Letter	Spaces in Line Length		Blank Lines Between Date and Inside Address	
	Elite	Pica	Elite	Pica
Under 100	50	40	7–9	5–7
100–200	60	50	5–7	3–5
200–300	70	60	3–4	3
Over 300 (two pages)	70	60	3	3

inside address in modified block letter

d. In the personal business letter, the inside address is placed after the closing lines. If the typed signature line is omitted, leave five or six blank lines after the complimentary close before beginning the inside address. If a typed signature line is included, leave two blank lines after the typed signature before beginning the inside address.

personal business letter without typed signature

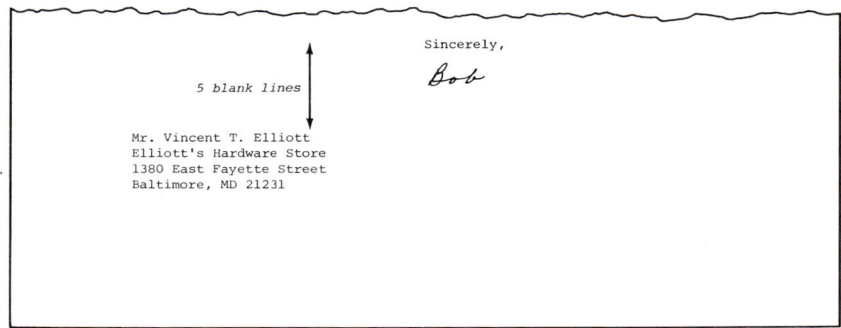

personal business letter with typed signature

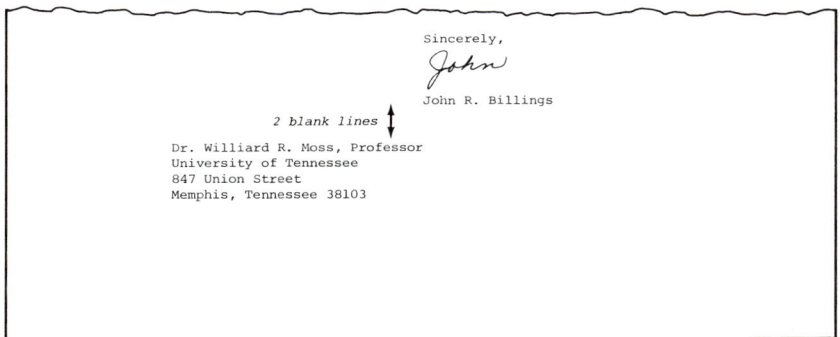

10-9. Attention Line

a. The attention line is used for directing correspondence to an individual or department within a company while still officially addressing the letter to the organization. In the modified block style, the attention line is placed at the left margin, centered, or indented to align with the paragraphs in the letter. Place the attention line a double space below the last line of the inside address. Use all capital letters or a combination of capital and lowercase letters underlined. The word *attention* may be typed with or without a colon following it.

attention line at left margin

```
                    Prescott Industries, Inc.
                    5450 North 37 Street
                    Tampa, Florida 33610

                    ATTENTION:   DR. JAMES MANOS
```

attention line centered

```
                    Phillips Bootery
                    3182 Jackson Street
                    San Francisco, CA 94115

                         Attention Ms. Sydney Corveau, Manager
```

attention line aligned with paragraph indentions

```
                    Freestone Rubber Company
                    1200 North Clybourn Avenue
                    Chicago, Illinois 60610

                         Attention Personnel Director

                    Gentlemen:

                         As accounts supervisor for a major industrial firm
                    in the Detroit area, I have had the opportunity to handle
                    transactions involving wholesalers throughout the country.
```

b.   In the full block letter style, the attention line is placed at the left margin a double space below the last line of the inside address. Use all capital letters or a combination of capital and lowercase letters underlined. The word *Attention* may or may not be followed by a colon.

```
                    SST Products, Inc.
                    840 30th Street
                    Boulder, CO 80303

                    ATTENTION ADJUSTMENT DEPARTMENT
```

10

c.   In the simplified letter style, the attention line is included in the inside address and is typed directly below the organization name. Treat the attention line as you would any other line in the inside address. The word *Attention* may or may not be followed by a colon. Some companies who use the modified or full block letter styles also prefer to treat the attention line in this manner and use the same format for the envelope address.

attention line included in inside address

```
Valley Manufacturing Company
Attention:  Ms. Karen Long, Manager
18692 Sierra Bonita Boulevard
San Bernardino, California 91783
```

10–10. Salutation

a. Type the salutation a double space below the last line of the inside address or the attention line, if used. Omit the salutation in the simplified letter style. Begin the salutation at the left margin for all other letter styles. In letters addressed to individuals, use one of the following salutations, depending upon the degree of formality desired. Use a colon after the salutation if mixed punctuation is used; use no punctuation mark if open punctuation is used.

informal salutation

Dear Fred: Dear Elsie:

standard business letter salutation to a single addressee

Dear Mr. Hampton: Dear Miss Baker:

Dear Ms. Harris: Dear Mrs. Chin:

standard business letter salutation to two men

Dear Mr. Hampton and Mr. Cranston:
    or
Dear Messrs. Hampton and Cranston:
    or
Gentlemen:

standard business letter salutation to two women

Dear Ms. Reed and Ms. Johnson:
    or
Dear Mses. Reed and Johnson:

standard business letter salutation to two single women

Dear Miss Frazier and Miss Goodlad:
    or
Dear Misses Frazier and Goodlad:

standard business letter salutation to two married women

Dear Mrs. Koonce and Mrs. O'Donnell:
    or
Dear Mesdames Koonce and O'Donnell:
    or
Mesdames:

10

standard business letter salutation to two persons with different courtesy titles

Dear Ms. Knott and Mr. Wade:

standard salutations to persons with professional titles

Dear Dr. Parsons:

Dear Professor Bredow:

Dear Colonel Jones:

formal salutations for certain government officials and religious dignitaries

Sir:

Excellency:

Reverend Sir:

Your Eminence:

b. If it is not known whether the addressee is a man or a woman, use the courtesy title *Mr.* or the full name of the person without a courtesy title. Use the courtesy title *Ms.* for a woman unless another title is specified by the addressee.

courtesy title "Mr."

Mr. Orolyn Ruenz (Dear Mr. Ruenz:)

Mr. Chris Meister (Dear Mr. Meister:)

Mr. J. T. Weyenberg (Dear Mr. Weyenberg:)

full name without courtesy title

Orolyn Ruenz (Dear Orolyn Ruenz:)

Chris Meister (Dear Chris Meister:)

J. T. Weyenberg (Dear J. T. Weyenberg:)

courtesy title for a woman

Ms. Sharon Reember (Dear Ms. Reember:)

Ms. Laura Nguyen (Dear Ms. Nguyen:)

10

c. In correspondence addressed to companies, associations, or other groups, use one of the following salutations:

salutations for groups composed of men and women*

Gentlemen: (most common)

Ladies and Gentlemen:

Gentlemen and Ladies:

---

*While advocated by some persons, the terms *Gentlepersons* and *Gentlepeople* have not yet achieved widespread acceptance in business.

salutation for groups composed entirely of men

Gentlemen:

salutations for groups composed entirely of women

Mesdames:

Ladies:

d. Letters addressed to a firm but directed to the attention of an individual within the company receive the salutation used to open a letter to a group: *Gentlemen, Ladies and Gentlemen, Gentlemen and Ladies, Mesdames,* or *Ladies.**

```
Grand Avenue Merchants Association
2834 Central Avenue, N.W.
Albuquerque, New Mexico 87105

ATTENTION MR. CORDAY WESTPHAL, PRESIDENT

Ladies and Gentlemen:
```

10–11. Subject Line

a. In the modified block style, begin the subject line at the left margin, center it, or align it with the paragraph indentions. Place it a double space below the salutation. The word *Subject* may or may not precede the line. If it is used, it is followed by a colon. Type the subject line in all capital letters or capital and lowercase letters underlined. If an attention line appears in the same letter, select the same typewritten form for both lines.

subject line at left margin

```
Gentlemen:

SUBJECT: HOURLY RATE INCREASE FOR EMPLOYEES
```

subject line centered

```
Dear Mr. Fanu:

        ANTICIPATED COST REDUCTIONS
```

---

*See 9–8, Forms of Address, for proper use of formal titles, salutations, and complimentary closings.

subject line aligned with paragraph indention

```
Dear Mr. Haley:

     Subject:  New Membership Applications

     Several prospective members have indicated an
interest in joining the women's assistance guild.
These women are interested in volunteer work . . .
```

attention and subject lines in the same letter

```
Attention Personnel Manager

Gentlemen:

Subject:  Insurance Benefits for Regular Employees
```

b. In the full block style, begin the subject line at the left margin a double space below the salutation. The word *Subject* may or may not precede the line. Type the subject line in all capital letters or capital and lowercase letters underlined. If an attention line appears in the same letter, select the same typewritten form for both lines.

```
ATTENTION ORDER DEPARTMENT

Gentlemen

PURCHASE ORDER 14978 DATED JUNE 28, 1979
```

c. In the simplified style the subject line replaces the salutation. Begin the subject line at the left margin a triple space below the inside address. Type it in all capital letters without the term *Subject*. Triple-space between the subject line and the first line of the body of the letter.

```
Mr. Jack Rochester, Editor
Wadsworth Publishing Company
10 Davis Drive
Belmont, California 94002


PURCHASE OF WORD PROCESSING EQUIPMENT


We appreciate receiving your letter inquiring about our new word processing
equipment.  Our salesman, Bill Retkoe, will be in the area soon, and he
```

10

d. Insurance and financial institutions, attorneys, and government offices often use the reference *Re:* or *In re:* in place of the word *Subject:*.

IN RE: TOLBERT VS. FEINBERG

Re: Policy 489–6342, Insured Michael T. Block

e. When initiating or replying to correspondence that has a special policy number, order number, or other such reference, include this information in a subject line (as illustrated in 10–11a–d) or in a specific reference below and aligned with the date. If references are not printed on the letterhead, use designations such as *When replying, refer to:, File No.:, In reply to:, Re:, Your reference:, Refer to:,* etc. These notations are typed a double space below the date or a double space below a personal or mailing notation appearing below the date.

below date

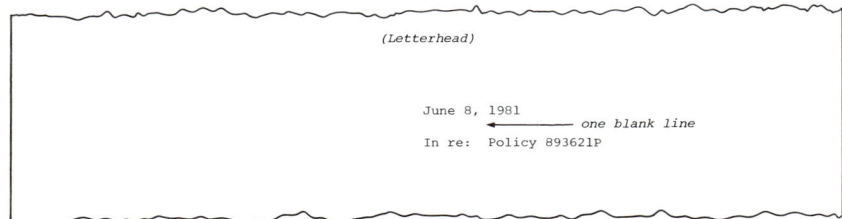

below personal or mailing notation

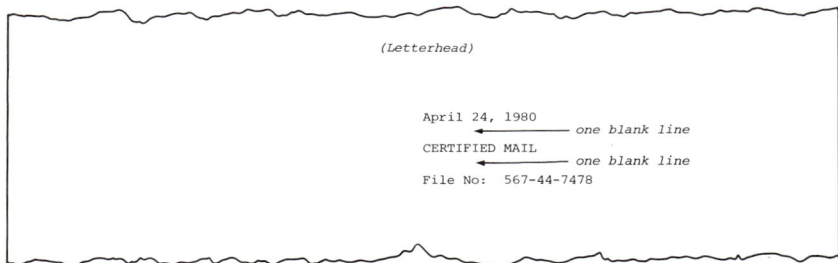

10 10–12. Body of the Letter

a. For the majority of business letters, single-space paragraphs within the body of the letter and double-space between each paragraph. For the modified block style with blocked paragraphs, the full block style, and the simplified style, begin each paragraph at the left margin. For the modified block style with indented paragraphs, indent the first line of each paragraph from five to ten typewritten spaces. Paragraphs may be either indented or blocked in the personal business letter style.

body of letter with blocked paragraphs

Dear Mr. Bedrosian:

Your Zippo portable radio arrived yesterday, along with
your explanation of the needed repairs.

As you suggested, the station tuning mechanism has been
replaced under the terms of the warranty. In examining
your radio, however, our serviceman noticed that the
speaker had been damaged from an apparent jarring or
dropping. The cost and installation of a new speaker
would be $15.98.

body of letter with indented paragraphs

Dear Mrs. Russell:

    We enjoyed the presentation on color coordination
that you gave to Dr. Halpern's secretarial workshop
last Saturday. Thank you for sharing your valuable
ideas with us.

    The class especially appreciated the material you
gave us on the Wilson color wheel. Everyone agreed
that this information will certainly be helpful in
making wardrobe selections for the office.

10

b. The body of letters consisting of one or two short paragraphs may be double-spaced using the modified block style with indented paragraphs or the personal business style with indented paragraphs.

short, one-paragraph letter

Connecticut Life Insurance Company

916 New Britain Avenue   Hartford, Connecticut 06106

Telephone: (203) 761-8211

July 27, 1979

Aaron, Aaron, & Cohen
Attorneys at Law
9324 Wilshire Boulevard
Beverly Hills, CA 90212

Gentlemen:

Our copy of the Bixby contract arrived today.

Thank you for forwarding it so promptly.

Sincerely yours,

Frances T. Archer
General Counsel

rn

10

short, two-paragraph letter

The Ironworks

2520 Eastern Avenue
Las Vegas, NE 89109

September 12, 1979

Mr. Perry Sneed, Manager
Green Thumb Nursery
3619 Kyrene Road
Tempe, Arizona 85282

Dear Mr. Sneed:

Your order for 3 dozen wrought iron potracks was shipped today.

We appreciate receiving Green Thumb Nursery as a new account. Thank you for your initial order, and we look forward to a pleasant business relationship.

Sincerely,

Lorraine Holloway
Sales Manager

fb

10–13. Complimentary Close

a. The complimentary close selected to end a business letter must comply with the formality of the salutation. Sample salutations as well as suitable complimentary closes are listed here.

Salutation	Complimentary Close

formal correspondence

Dear Mr. President	Very truly yours
His Excellency	Sincerely yours
Dear Senator Monroe	

general business correspondence

Dear Mr. Siebert	Sincerely yours
Dear Ms. Mendoza	Sincerely
Gentlemen	

informal business correspondence

Dear Bill	Sincerely yours
Dear Karen	Sincerely
	Cordially yours
	Cordially

b. In the modified block styles and the personal business style, the complimentary close is typed a double space below the last line of the body. Begin the closing (1) at the page center, (2) five spaces to the left of the page center, or (3) aligned with the longest closing line that has been back-spaced from the right margin.

complimentary close begun at page center

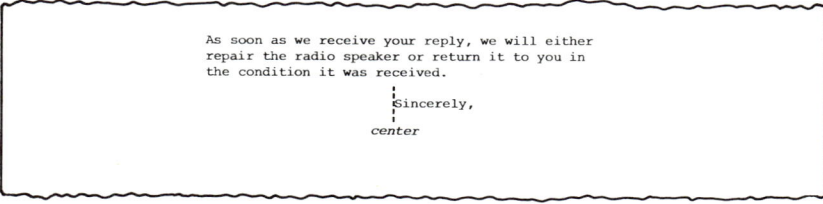

194

complimentary close begun five spaces to the left of page center

> We would appreciate receiving your check within
> the next week so that we can mark your account
> "paid."
>
>   Sincerely yours,
>
>   *center*

complimentary close aligned with closing line back-spaced from right margin

> Don't delay; act now to receive a copy of Your
> Banking Future--while the supply lasts.
>
>   Sincerely yours,
>
>   BARCLAY TRAINING INSTITUTE
>
>
>   Morgan Barclay, Director

c. In the full block letter style, the complimentary close is typed at the left margin a double space below the last line of the body.

> May I please have an opportunity to review my
> qualifications with you? Just call me at
> 349-8211, and I will be pleased to come to
> your office for an interview.
>
> Sincerely yours,

d. No complimentary close is used in the simplified letter style.

10

10–14. Signature Lines

a. Some business firms include the name of the company in the signature lines. In such cases the name of the company is typed in all capital letters a double space below the complimentary close. The first letter of the company name is aligned with the first letter of the complimentary close. Company signature lines are not used in the personal and simplified letter styles.

modified block letter

```
                              Sincerely yours,

                              GREENBAY TRAVEL AGENCY
```

full block letter

```
              Sincerely yours,

              REDVIEW TILE COMPANY
```

b. In the modified and full block letter styles, begin typing the name and title of the person writing the letter on the fourth blank line below the complimentary close or the company name, whichever line is lower. Align the first letter of the individual's name with the first letter of the company name or the complimentary close.

full block letter

```
        Sincerely,


        Lewis A. List
        Vice-President
```

modified block letter

```
                      Sincerely yours,

                      FIRST NATIONAL BANK


                      David L. Satilow, Manager
                      Trust Department
```

c. Type combinations of names and titles so that balance is achieved in the signature lines. The name and title may appear on the same line or on separate lines, depending upon the length of each item.

single-line typed signature

Philip Ashton, President

two-line typed signatures

Wilma T. Washington
Manager, Accounting Department

John S. Ross, Manager
Data Processing Department

Horace F. Tavelman
Accounts and Sales Representative

three-line typed signature

Roberta Casselman
Senior Film Editor
Division of Secondary Education

d. Signature lines containing the names of men are not preceded by the courtesy title *Mr.* Signature lines containing the names of women are not preceded by a courtesy title unless the writer prefers to make the distinction of *Ms., Mrs.,* or *Miss.* The title may or may not be placed in parentheses.

signature lines containing name of man

George R. Bezowski
Regional Manager

signature lines containing name of woman

Mary R. Stevens
Regional Manager
        or
Ms. Mary R. Stevens   (Ms.) Mary R. Stevens
Regional Manager   Regional Manager
        or
Miss Mary R. Stevens   (Miss) Mary R. Stevens
Regional Manager   Regional Manager
        or
Mrs. Mary R. Stevens   (Mrs.) Mary R. Stevens
Regional Manager   Regional Manager

e. Correspondence that is signed by a person other than the one whose name appears in the typed signature line usually shows the initials of the person signing the letter.

f. In the simplified letter style, the entire signature line is typed in all capital letters on a single line. It begins at the left margin on the fifth line below the last line of the message.

```
appreciate receiving your reply within the next week.



JOANN STEVENS, ASSISTANT TO THE VICE-PRESIDENT
```

g. In the personal business style, the typed signature line may be omitted. If it is included, only the individual's name, not title, is written.

typed signature line omitted

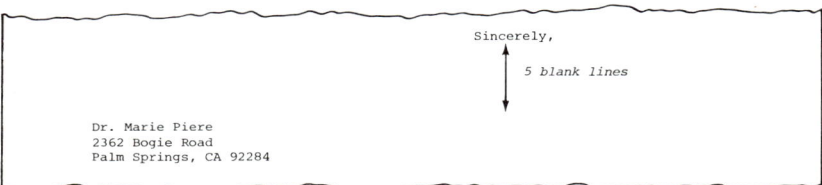

```
                                        Sincerely,

                                            ↑
                                            │  5 blank lines
                                            ↓
        Dr. Marie Piere
        2362 Bogie Road
        Palm Springs, CA 92284
```

typed signature line included

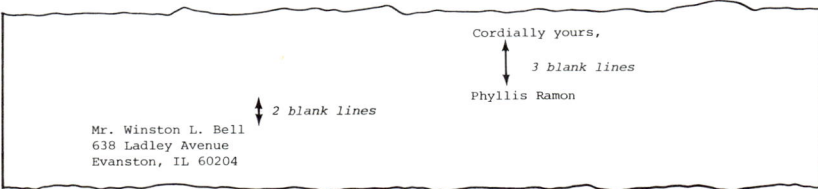

```
                                        Cordially yours,
                                            ↑
                                            │  3 blank lines
                                        Phyllis Ramon
            ↕ 2 blank lines
        Mr. Winston L. Bell
        638 Ladley Avenue
        Evanston, IL 60204
```

10–15. Reference Initials

10

a. Except in the personal business style, reference initials are used to show who typed the letter. The typist's initials are typed in lowercase letters at the left margin a double space (or single space in longer letters) below the last line in the signature block.

```
                                        Sincerely yours,


                                        Nancy L. Cole
                                        Superintendent

        rt
```

b. Both the initials of the dictator and the typist may be included in the reference notation. When the person who has signed the letter is the one who dictated it, his initials appear in capital letters before the typist's initials. The initials are separated by a colon or a diagonal line.

```
                                      Sincerely yours,

                                      JAMESTOWN PLUMBING SUPPLY


                                      Owen F. Toburg, Manager
                   OFT:md
```

c. When correspondence is written by a person other than the one whose signature appears in the typed signature line, the dictator's initials in capital letters or his name precedes the initials of the typist. Separate the initials or name of the dictator from the typist's initials by a colon or a diagonal line.

```
                                        Sincerely yours,


                                        Stephen T. Pendleton
                                        President
                      KWashburn/rt
```

10-16. Enclosure or Attachment Notations

a. If any enclosures are included with the letter, an enclosure notation is typed a double space (or single space in longer letters) below the reference initials. Place the enclosure notation at the left margin. Following are some examples of enclosure notations:

Enclosures: Check for $20   2 Enclosures
             Copy of Invoice 1362

Enc.   Enclosure   Enclosures 3   Enc. 2

b. When an enclosure is attached to the letter, the word *Attachment* or its abbreviation may be used in place of the enclosure notation.

Attachments: Application for admission   Attachment
              Student information form

Att.   Att.: 2   Attachments 2

10–17. Carbon Copy Notations

a. When carbon copies of correspondence are directed to other individuals, note the distribution at the bottom of the letter. The carbon copy notation is typed a double space (or single space in longer letters) below the enclosure notation, if used; otherwise, a single or double space below the reference initials. However, if a mailing notation follows the reference initials or enclosure notation, the carbon copy notation is typed below it. Carbon copy notations may include a combination of the courtesy title, name, position, company, and complete address of an individual. Following are some examples of appropriate carbon copy notations:

cc: Mr. John R. Robinson

CC: Francis P. Olsen, President, Wilson Corporation

cc Alice Morley, Credit Clerk

CC Gene Rupe

carbon copy notation following reference initials

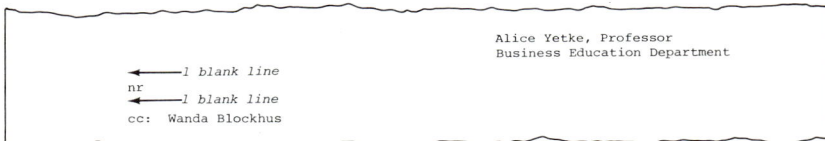

carbon copy notation with additional notations

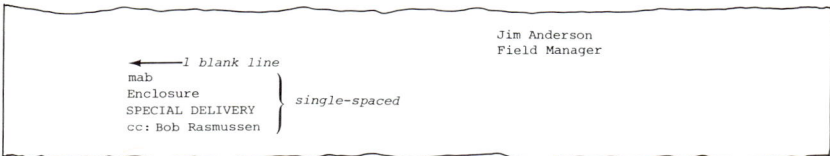

b. In some cases copies are made on a copying machine rather than with carbon paper. Some companies note these copies in the following way:

copy: Ms. Janice Welch

copies: Bill Acevedo
       Donna Mellert

copy to Mr. Bill Hughes, Manager, Hillsdale Paper Corporation

c. If copies are directed to more than one individual, list the individuals according to rank. If the individuals are equal in rank or ranking is unimportant, alphabetize the list.

ranked list

cc: R. F. Gillham, President
    T. L. McMillan, Vice-President
    F. S. Simpkins, General Manager

alphabetized list

cc Marcus L. Brendero, Adam S. Langville, David M. Silverman

d. If it is unnecessary or inappropriate for an addressee to know that a copy or copies of the letter are being sent to other individuals, use a blind carbon copy notation.

To do this, position the carriage where you wish to begin typing. Then, disengage the paper release lever and carefully remove the original without disturbing the carbon pack. Return the paper release lever to the lock position and type the blind carbon copy notation so that the first copy and all others will contain the notation. The blind carbon copy notation may be typed (1) on the seventh line from the top of the page at the left margin or (2) where the regular copy notation normally appears.

bcc: Bruce R. Caldwell

bcc Ms. Miriam Minkoff

10–18. Postscripts

A postscript may be used to add an idea that was inadvertently omitted from the body of the letter or an idea that requires emphasis. The postscript appears in last position; it may be typed or handwritten with or without the abbreviation *P.S.* If typewritten, leave a blank line between the previous letter part and the postscript.

with abbreviation "P.S."

without abbreviation "P.S."

```
JNT/rpn
cc:  Ellen Anderson, Kathleene Basil, Sylvia Cohen

Don't miss the opportunity to order Living World Today.
Remember that this offer ends October 31!
```

```
JNT/rpn

CC Joyce Mason, Leo Sirakides, Agnes Steebing
```

Don't miss the opportunity to order Living World Today. Remember that this offer ends October 31!

10–19. Second-Page Headings

a. Type headings for second and succeeding pages on plain paper. Begin typing on the seventh line, using the same margins that appear on the first page. These page headings include the name of the addressee, the page number, and the date. Either a horizontal or vertical format may be used.

horizontal format

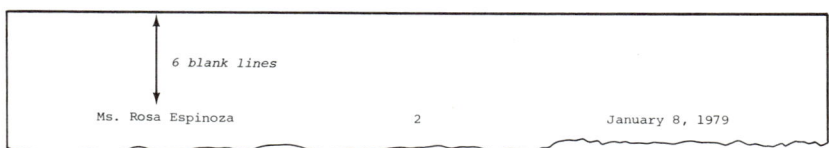

```
            ↑
            6 blank lines
            ↓

Ms. Rosa Espinoza                    2              January 8, 1979
```

vertical format

```
            ↑
            6 blank lines
            ↓

Ms. Rosa Espinoza
Page 2
Jaunary 8, 1979
```

b. Before resuming the message, space down three lines from the last line of the heading.

c. Do not divide the last word on the previous page, and include at least two lines of a new paragraph at the bottom. Likewise, at least two lines from a paragraph need to be carried forward to any additional page. Leave from six to nine blank lines at the bottom of each page, except, of course, for the last one.

d. The closing lines of a business letter should not be isolated on a continuation page. At least two lines of the message must precede the complimentary close or signature line (when no complimentary close is used).

10

Punctuation Style

10–20. Mixed Punctuation

The most popular punctuation style for business letters is mixed punctuation. In this format a colon is placed after the salutation and a comma after the complimentary close. No other closing punctuation marks are used except those appearing within the body of the letter.

Dickens Crystal, Inc.

1640 Grand Boulevard
Schenectady, New York 12309
Telephone: (518) 872-3100

April 17, 1980

House of Imports
5700 Oxford Avenue
Philadelphia, PA 19149

Attention Ms. Jody Stevens, Buyer

Gentlemen:

Our complete line of Dickens Crystal is illustrated in the enclosed catalog. As you will note from the full-page color illustrations, its simple design and exquisite workmanship have made Dickens crystal one of the most popular lines in the country.

We appreciate your interest in our products and would be pleased to have the House of Imports carry them. I am sure you would find these fast-selling gift items a profitable addition to your inventory.

A complete list of prices and the terms of sale are included in the back pages of the catalog. You will also note that we serve you by providing a breakage credit up to 5 percent of purchases on merchandise displayed in your store. Just return any broken pieces, and we will replace the merchandise.

We hope that we can add your name to the many retailers throughout the country who represent Dickens crystal. Should you wish to open an account with us, please return the enclosed credit application forms. If you wish to place a c.o.d. order, we can deliver the merchandise within ten days of the receipt of your order.

Let Dickens start earning for you today.

Sincerely,

Edward T. Cowan
Vice-President, Marketing

ma
Enclosures

10

10–21. Open Punctuation

Writers of business letters often use open punctuation. No closing punctuation marks appear after the letter parts. The only ending punctuation marks are those used within the body of the letter.

Gibraltar Insurance Company of America

916 New Britain Avenue
Hartford, Connecticut 06106
Telephone: (203) 743-1200

June 16, 1979

Lynch & Marten Insurance Agency
16320 San Fernando Mission Boulevard
Sepulveda, California 91343

Gentlemen

SUBJECT: CLAIM NO. AT 6509, INSURED THOMAS A. GLASCO

The claim of your client, Mr. Thomas A. Glasco, for $300 to replace the golf clubs that were stolen from him in Las Vegas is covered under his homeowner's policy, No. 19362084.

To process Mr. Glasco's claim, we must have a copy of the police report filed at the time of the theft. Please contact the police agency handling the theft report and have them forward us a copy addressed to my attention.

As soon as we receive the necessary information, Mr. Glasco's check will be sent to your office.

Sincerely yours

GIBRALTAR INSURANCE COMPANY OF AMERICA

Mariam R. Marsh, Claims Adjuster

fd

cc: Mr. Thomas A. Glasco

10

Addressing Envelopes

10–22. Return Address

a. The return address is usually printed in the upper left corner of the envelope. In large companies the initiator's initials or name and location are typed above the company name and return address. This practice facilitates routing the letter to the sender in case of nondelivery by the post office.

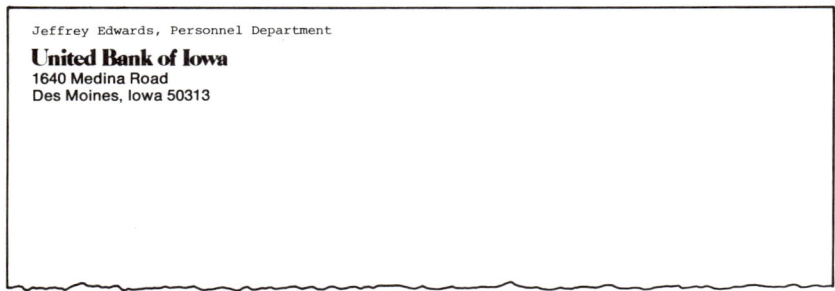

```
Jeffrey Edwards, Personnel Department
United Bank of Iowa
1640 Medina Road
Des Moines, Iowa 50313
```

b. On an envelope without a printed return address, type the return address in the upper left corner. Single-space the typewritten lines and include (1) the name of the individual or the individual and the company; (2) the mailing address; and (3) the city, state, and zip code. Begin typing on the third line from the top of the envelope and on the fourth space from the left edge.

```
            ↕ 2 blank lines
John R. Stevens
460 Old Dorsett Road
Hazelwood, MO 63043
↑
3 blank spaces
```

10–23. Mailing Address

a. Single-space the mailing address, using at least two lines. The last line of the address should contain the city, state, and zip code. If the envelope is used to mail correspondence, type the address exactly as it appears in the inside address.

b. On No. 10 envelopes (4½ by 9½ inches) space down to line 12 or 13. Begin typing the address 4 to 4½ inches from the left edge, depending upon the line length of the mailing address.

No. 10 envelope

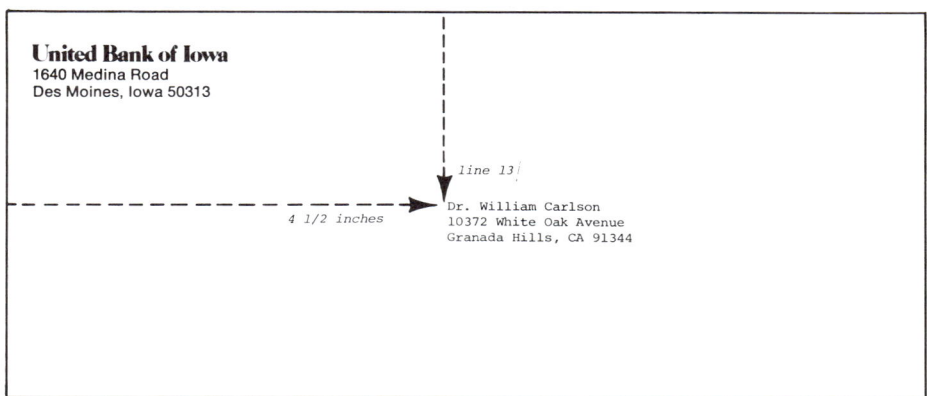

c. On No. 6¾ envelopes (3⅝ by 6½ inches) space down to line 11 or 12. Begin typing the mailing address 2 to 2½ inches from the left edge, depending upon the line length of the mailing address.

No. 6¾ envelope

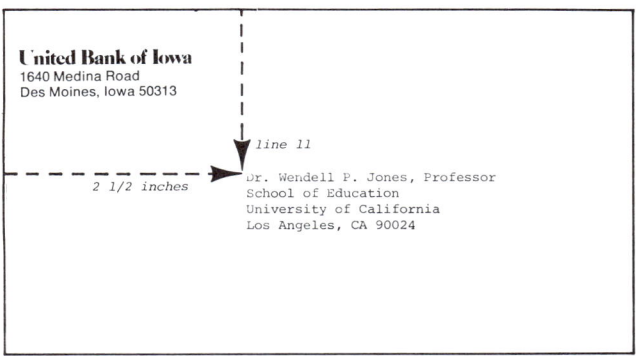

d. No. 7 (3⅞ by 7½ inches) and No. 5⅛ (4⅝ by 5 15/16 inches) envelopes are used less frequently than the standard No. 10 and No. 6¾ envelopes. On No. 7 envelopes, space down to line 12; on No. 5⅛ envelopes, space down to line 14. Begin typing the mailing address ½ to 1 inch left of the envelope center, depending upon the length of the address lines.

10

No. 7 envelope

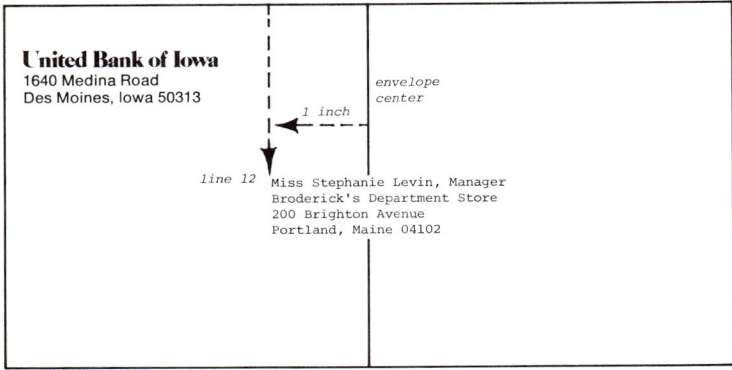

No. 5⅛ envelope

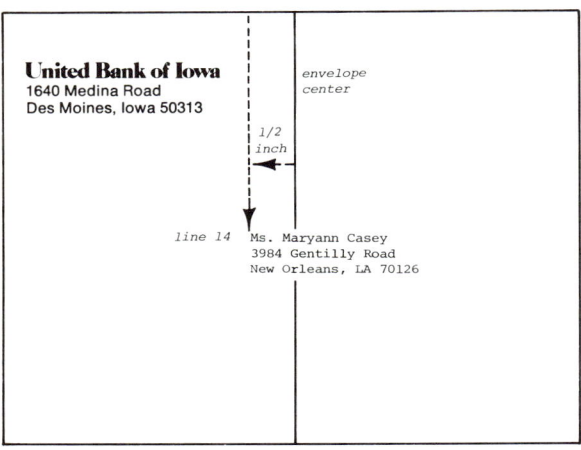

e. Letter-size manila envelopes (9 by 12 inches or 10 by 12 inches) may have the address typed directly on the envelope or have a label with the address affixed to the envelope. In either case, the first line of the mailing address is placed 6 inches from the top edge of the envelope. Locate the address from 1 to 1½ inches left of the envelope center, depending upon the length of the address lines.

letter-size manila envelope

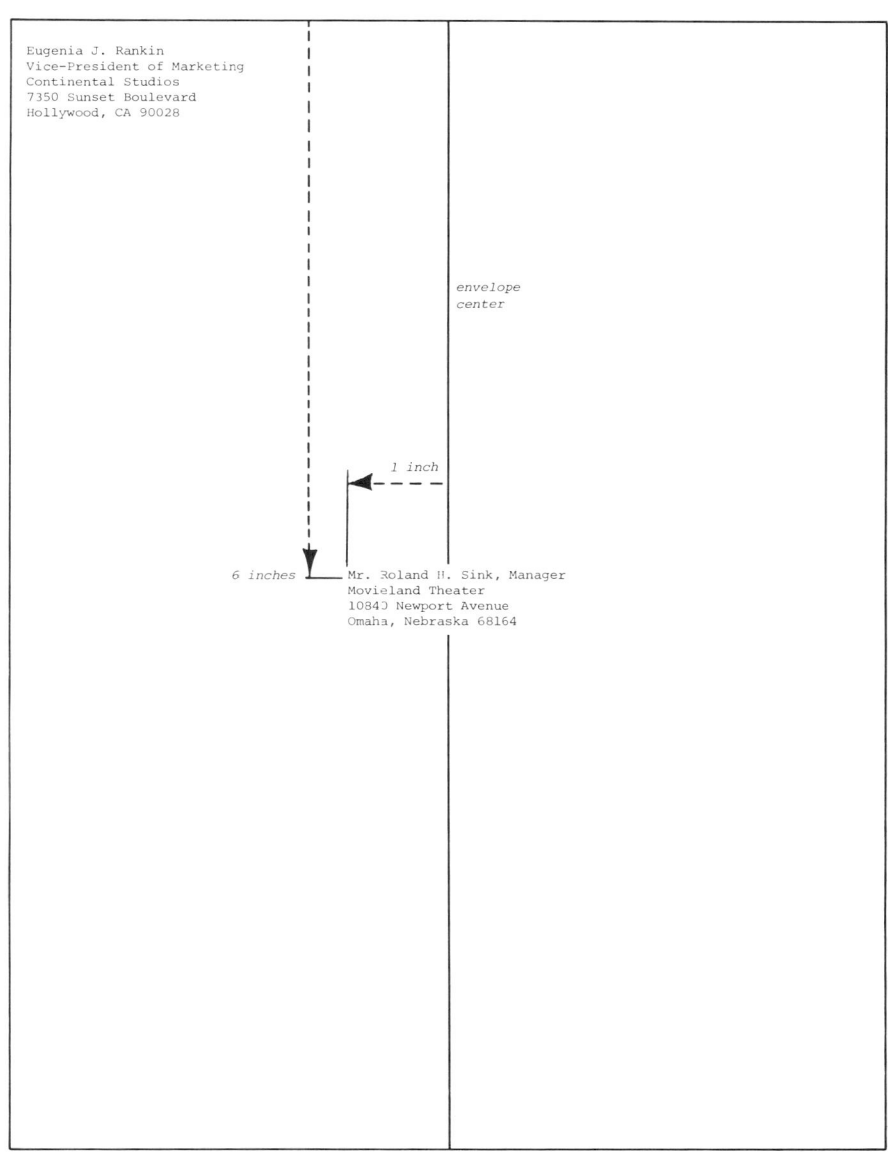

Eugenia J. Rankin
Vice-President of Marketing
Continental Studios
7350 Sunset Boulevard
Hollywood, CA 90028

*envelope
center*

1 inch

6 inches

Mr. Roland H. Sink, Manager
Movieland Theater
10840 Newport Avenue
Omaha, Nebraska 68164

10

10–24. Special Notations

a. Type an attention line or a special notation such as *Personal* or *Confidential* a double space below the last line of the return address or 1½ inches (line 9 for standard typewriters) from the top edge of the envelope, whichever position is lower. Use capital and lowercase letters and underline the notation.

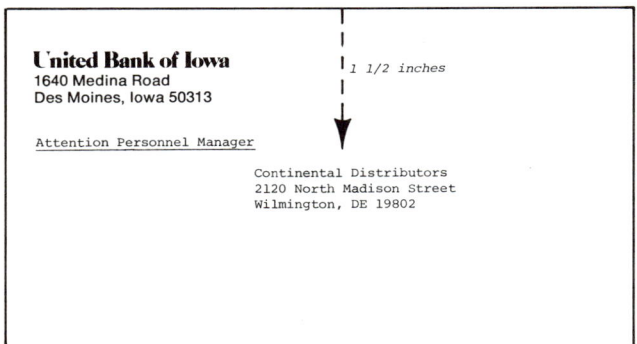

b. If an attention line is included with the mailing address instead of typed on a separate line, place it directly below the organizational name.

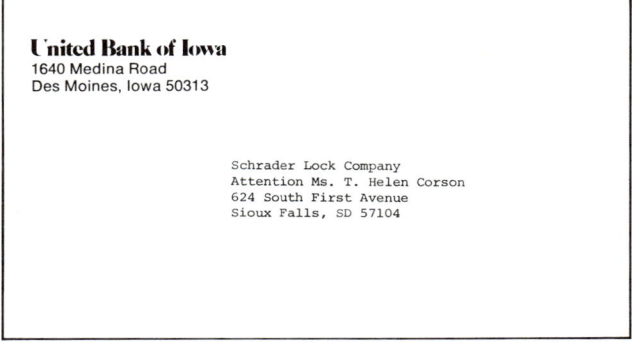

10–25. Mailing Notations

Type mailing notations such as *Airmail* (for foreign destinations), *Special Delivery, Certified Mail,* or *Registered Mail* in all capital letters below the stamp, 1½ inches (line 9 for standard typewriters) from the top edge of the envelope.

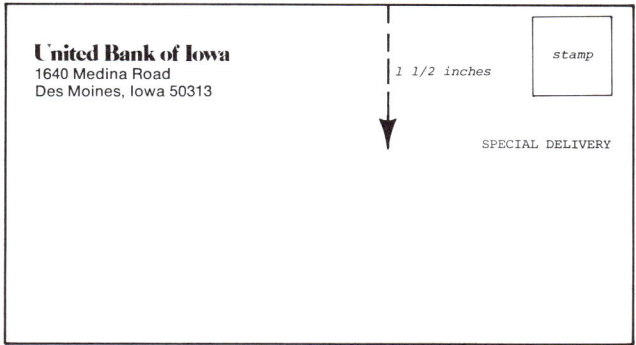

10–26. Addressing Envelopes for Faster Processing

In 1972 the U.S. Post Office introduced a format for faster handling of mail addressed by plates or computerized equipment (Customer Services Publication 59). This publication was updated in 1975. In a 1974 publication (Customer Services Notice 23–B) and again in a 1977 publication (Customer Services Publication 62), the U.S. Post Office recommended that a similar addressing format be used for all other mail.

For general business correspondence most companies still prefer the formality of using the same form of address for both the inside address and the envelope. This format is described in 10–23 through 10–25. If a company follows the U.S. Post Office recommendations, however, use the following guidelines for addressing all mail.

a. Addresses should be placed at least 1 inch from the left edge of the envelope. The bottom of the last line should be at least ⅝ of an inch from the bottom edge of the envelope. Keep the lower right half of the envelope free of printing or symbols.

b. Use block-style type fonts (no italics, script, artistic, or proportionately spaced fonts) and type addresses in uppercase letters without punctuation. The address area on all mailed materials should be blocked, with all lines having uniform left margins.

c. The bottom line of the address should include the city, state, and zip code in that sequence. The names of cities may be abbreviated. Use the two-letter state abbreviation separated from the zip code by only a single space.

DALLAS TX 75201

CY OF INDUSTRY CA 90014

d. The delivery point for the mail, whether it is a street address or a box number, must be shown on the second line from the bottom, directly above the city, state, and zip code. When apartment numbers, suite numbers, room numbers, etc., are used, they should be placed immediately after the street address on the same line.

When mail is addressed to a box number, place first the station name and then the box number both on the same line. If this combination is too long, the station name may be shown on the preceding line.

street address

8325 W HALBY ST APT 27
DENVER CO 80202

box number with station name

JEFFERSON STN PO BOX 3302
DETROIT MI 48214

e. Attention lines may be shown on any line of the address block above the second line from the bottom. The attention line is usually typed directly following the organization name.

GENERAL MANUFACTURING COMPANY
ATTENTION MR EDWARD R KING
JEFFERSON STN PO BOX 3302
DETROIT MI 48214

f. Account numbers, subscription numbers, presort codes, etc., may be located within the address block. Such numbers are typed immediately above the addressee's name.

973-81269346
MS ROBERTA W FRANK
8325 W HALBY ST APT 27
DENVER CO 80202

10 | Folding and Inserting Correspondence

10-27. No. 10 and No. 7 Envelopes

a. Fold up one-third of the page.

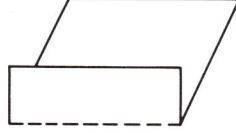

b.   Fold down the upper third of the page so that the top edge is approximately ½ inch above the first fold.

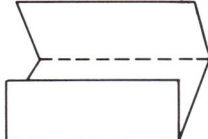 

c.   Insert the page so that the top edge is near the top edge of the envelope.

10–28.   No. 6¾ Envelopes

a.   Fold up one-half of the page so that the bottom edge is approximately ½ inch below the top edge.

b.   From the right side fold over one-third of the page.

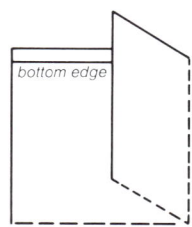

10

c. Fold over the second third of the page so that the left edge is approximately ½ inch from the right fold.

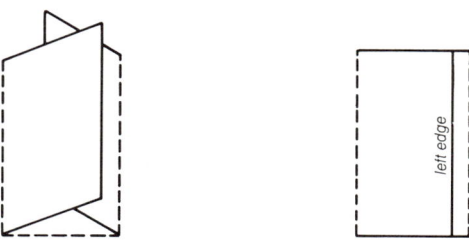

d. Insert the page so that the left edge is near the top edge of the envelope.

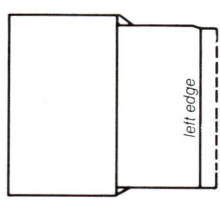

10–29. Window Envelopes

a. Fold up one-third of the letter.

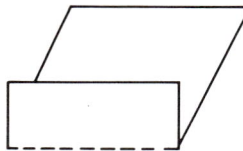

b. Turn the folded letter face down.

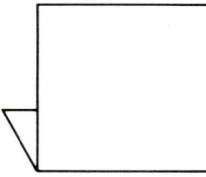

c. Fold down the upper third of the letter so that the top edge meets the first fold.

d.   Insert the letter so that the address appears in the window of the envelope.

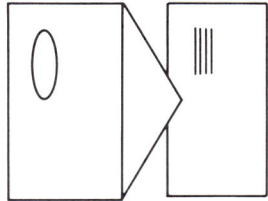

Memorandums

10–30.   Usage

Letters generally involve the transmission of written messages sent outside an organization. Written messages sent within the organization, however, more often take the form of a memorandum. Memorandums comprise the major medium for internal written communication.

10–31.   Preparation

a.   Procedures for preparing memorandums vary widely from office to office, but there are a few general guidelines. Most organizations have prepared forms for typing memorandums. These forms contain printed headings for directing the message to the addressee, designating the source of the message, indicating the date written, and identifying the subject content. While the arrangement and design may vary, these basic ingredients are found in most printed memorandum forms.

printed memorandum form

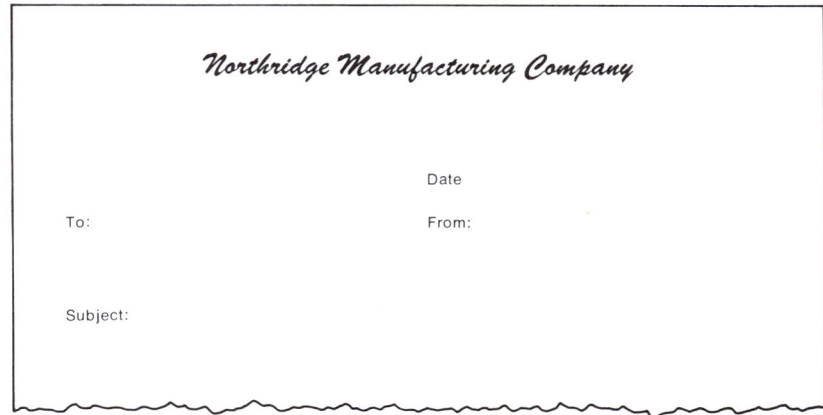

b. Some companies do not have standardized forms for typing memorandums. In these cases, use the following procedures for typing the memorandum on plain paper or paper containing the company letterhead.

   (1) A memorandum is usually typed on 8½-by-11-inch paper. For short memorandums, however, a half sheet (8½ by 5½ inches) is often used.

   (2) Type the date 2 inches (line 13) from the top of the paper. The date may be typed at the left margin, centered, begun at the center of the page, or be back-spaced from the right margin. Double- or triple-space after the date.

typewritten memorandum

Northridge Manufacturing Company

6201 Winnetka Avenue   Woodland Hills, California 91364
Telephone: (213) 347-0551

April 24, 1980

TO: All Employees

FROM: Donna Anderson, President

SUBJECT: Group Health Insurance

As you know, Stanley Hutchinson, your employee representative, proposed to the Board of Directors last January that we consider adopting an employee group health insurance plan. He pointed out the many medical expenses incurred by our employees throughout the year and the benefits a group health insurance policy would have in helping meet some of the medical expenses resulting from sickness and injuries.

After careful study of several group health insurance policies, the board concluded that the group policy proposed by the Edgewater Insurance Company would give the most comprehensive medical coverage for its cost. As a result, the board voted unanimously to adopt this policy, at no cost to the employees, effective June 1.

Attached is a brochure that explains in detail the health care services covered by the Edgewater policy. If you have any questions, please call Don Curry at Extension 7351. He will be glad to assist you.

rm

10

(3) Type in all capital letters and double-space the headings TO:, FROM:, and SUBJECT: at the left margin.

(4) Align the information following the headings two spaces after the SUBJECT: heading.

(5) Triple-space after SUBJECT: and begin typing the body of the memorandum. Single-space the message, but double-space between paragraphs. For short, one-paragraph memorandums, the body may be double-spaced.

c. When a memorandum contains more than one page, the heading for the second and succeeding pages should have a 1-inch margin from the top edge of the page. Show the name of the person to whom the memorandum is addressed, the page number, and the date. This information may be arranged vertically at the left margin or be placed on a single line with the name beginning at the left margin, the page number centered, and the date back-spaced from the right margin. Triple-space after the heading before continuing the body of the memorandum.

second-page headings

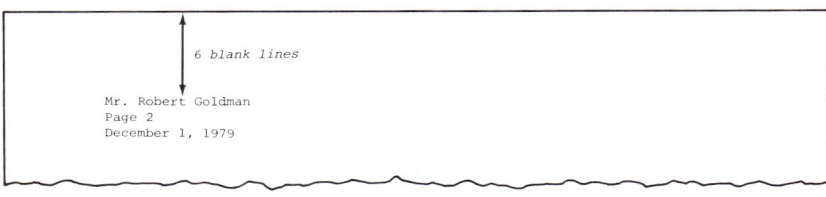

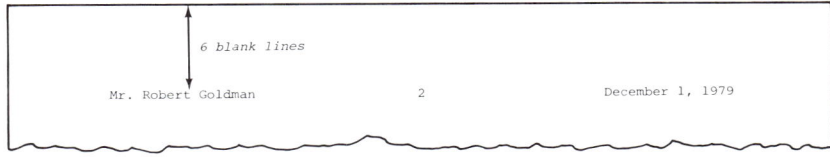

11
REPORTS AND MANUSCRIPTS

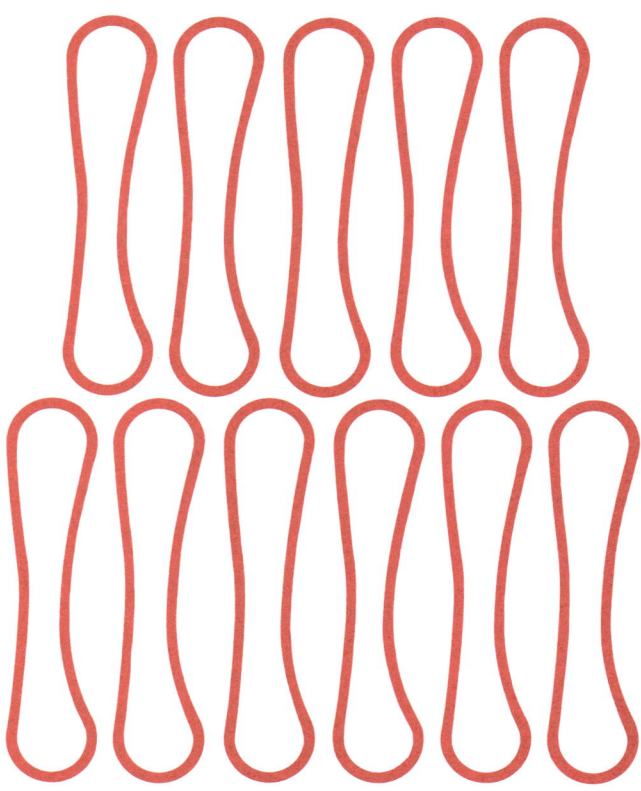

11

Reports and Manuscripts Solution Finder

11

Title Page

11–1. Content

The title page will generally contain (1) the name or title of the report or manuscript; (2) the name or name and title of the person, group, or organization for whom it was written; (3) the name and title of the person or group who wrote it; and (4) the date it was submitted. The contents of a title page are not restricted to these items.

11–2. Format

The title of the report or manuscript should be typed in all capital letters and centered 2 inches from the top of the paper. Allow a 2-inch bottom margin, and space equally the items appearing between the top and bottom margins. All items appearing on the title page should be centered. An illustration of a title page is on page 222.

Letter of Transmittal

11–3. Content

The letter of transmittal is used to introduce the reader to the report or manuscript. Although the content of the transmittal letter will depend upon the complexity and scope of the report or manuscript, it should basically tell the reader (1) what the topic is, (2) why the report was written, (3) how the report was compiled (method of research), (4) who worked on it or helped with its development, and (5) what major findings or conclusions resulted (if a synopsis or summary page is not included).

11–4. Format

The letter of transmittal should be friendly and concise, usually concluding with the writer showing appreciation for the opportunity to do the report or manuscript. It appears directly after the title page and may be typed in any acceptable business letter format. An illustration of a letter of transmittal is on page 223.

Table of Contents

11

11–5. Content and Format

The content and format of a table of contents depend upon the length and complexity of the report or manuscript but are usually prepared in the following way:

(1) Type the heading TABLE OF CONTENTS or CONTENTS in all capital letters centered 2 inches from the top edge of the paper.

(2) Type *Page* a triple space below the table of contents heading, back-spaced from the right margin (set 1¼ inches from the right edge of the paper).

(3) Type in all capital letters and double-space the preliminary sections of the report (i.e. letter of transmittal, list of tables, list of interviews). Begin a double space below *Page* and 1¼ inches from the left edge of the paper

title page

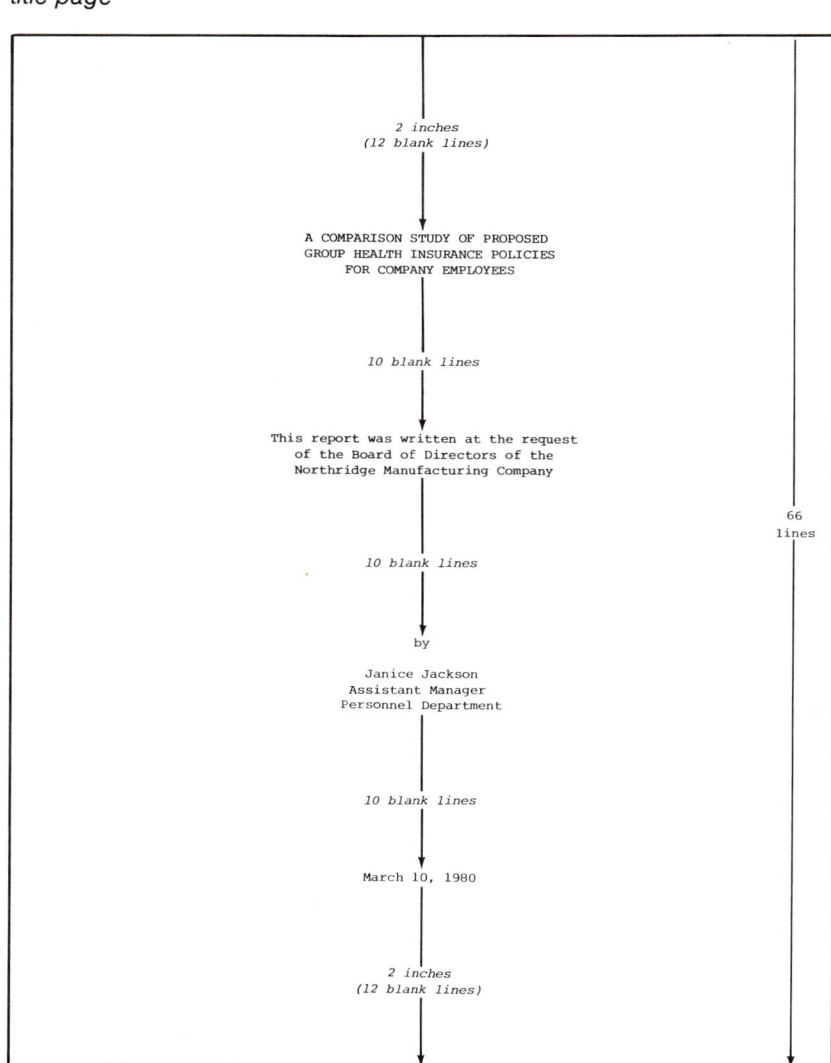

2 inches
(12 blank lines)

A COMPARISON STUDY OF PROPOSED
GROUP HEALTH INSURANCE POLICIES
FOR COMPANY EMPLOYEES

10 blank lines

This report was written at the request
of the Board of Directors of the
Northridge Manufacturing Company

66
lines

10 blank lines

by

Janice Jackson
Assistant Manager
Personnel Department

10 blank lines

March 10, 1980

2 inches
(12 blank lines)

11

(the left margin). Although it is paginated, the table of contents is not included in this listing. Number preliminary pages consecutively in lowercase roman numerals ½ inch from the bottom of the page. Count the title page as page i even though no number is shown on that page.

(4) Begin the major division heading of the report (i.e., chapter, section, unit, topic) at the left margin. The major division heading may either appear on

letter of transmittal

Northridge Manufacturing Company

6201 Winnetka Avenue   Woodland Hills, California 91364
Telephone: (213) 347-0551

March 10, 1980

Mr. Don Washington, President
Northridge Manufacturing Company
402 West Main Street
Northridge, Illinois 60162

Dear Mr. Washington:

As requested by our Board of Directors, here is the report comparing the employee group health insurance policies that were submitted by eight companies.

The policies were compared in the following ways:

    1. Company cost per employee
    2. Cost to employees
    3. Kinds of illnesses and/or injuries covered
    4. Hospital, out-patient, and home-visit coverage
    5. Total annual health benefits allowed
    6. Miscellaneous coverages such as medicines, X rays,
       physical therapy, private nursing, etc.
    7. Family members covered

As shown by the summary table on page 19, the Edgewater policy is superior in all categories except one--company cost per employee. I recommend we select the Edgewater proposal. The additional $3.16 annual cost per employee is relatively small considering the substantial benefits over any one of the other less expensive policies.

Thank you for the opportunity to conduct this study. I appreciate the help and cooperation I received from the employees' representative and from the representatives of the insurance companies.

If you have any questions or if I can be of further help, please let me know.

               Sincerely,

               Janice Jackson

               Janice Jackson, Assistant Manager
               Personnel Department

ba

11

the same line as *Page* or be typed a double space below the preliminary parts.

(5) Beginning at the left margin, type the major sections of the report in all capital letters. Those sections of lesser degree should be indented, typed in capital and lowercase letters, and placed in the same sequence as they appear in the report.

(6) Major sections of a report may be numbered by using uppercase roman numerals. Type the longest numeral at the left margin and indent the shorter numerals so the periods following the numerals are aligned.

(7) Use leaders (a line of alternating periods and spaces) to assist the reader in locating the page number of a particular section. While all major headings should have corresponding page numbers, it is not necessary to assign page numbers to subheadings appearing in the table of contents.

11

table of contents

TABLE OF CONTENTS

iii

11

11-6. List of Tables

When a report or manuscript contains several tables, it is often helpful as a reference to the reader to include a list of tables after the table of contents. The format for the list of tables is as follows:

(1) Type the heading LIST OF TABLES in all capital letters centered 2 inches from the top edge of the paper.

(2) Triple-space after the list of tables heading, and type *Table* at the left margin and *Page* back-spaced from the right margin.

(3) Indent three spaces from the left margin and type the number of each table followed by its title in all capital letters.

(4) Use leaders (a line of alternating periods and spaces) to assist the reader in locating the page number of a particular table.

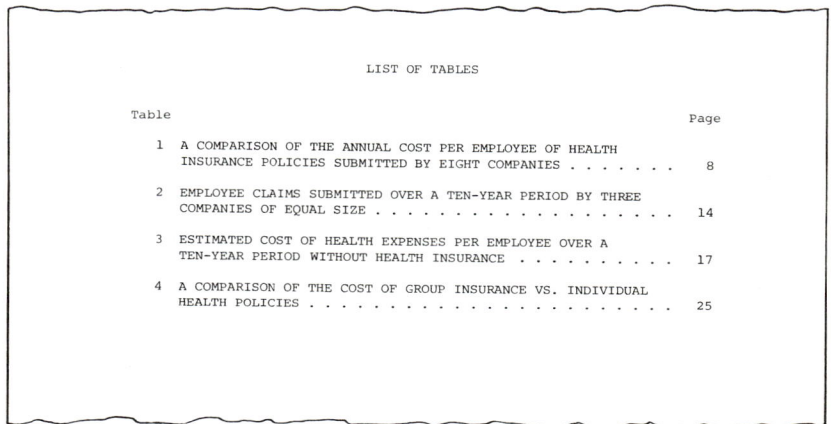

```
                              LIST OF TABLES

      Table                                                         Page

        1   A COMPARISON OF THE ANNUAL COST PER EMPLOYEE OF HEALTH
            INSURANCE POLICIES SUBMITTED BY EIGHT COMPANIES . . . . . . .   8

        2   EMPLOYEE CLAIMS SUBMITTED OVER A TEN-YEAR PERIOD BY THREE
            COMPANIES OF EQUAL SIZE . . . . . . . . . . . . . . . . . . .   14

        3   ESTIMATED COST OF HEALTH EXPENSES PER EMPLOYEE OVER A
            TEN-YEAR PERIOD WITHOUT HEALTH INSURANCE . . . . . . . . . .   17

        4   A COMPARISON OF THE COST OF GROUP INSURANCE VS. INDIVIDUAL
            HEALTH POLICIES . . . . . . . . . . . . . . . . . . . . . . .   25
```

Body of the Report

11–7. Typing the Report or Manuscript

a. Use the following margins for typing reports and manuscripts:

(1) A 1¼-inch left and right margin. When the report or manuscript will be bound, allow 1½ inches for the left margin.

(2) A 1-inch top margin for all pages except those with first-degree headings. Pages with first-degree headings have 2-inch top margins.

(3) A 1- to 1½-inch bottom margin. Allow at least two lines of a paragraph to appear at the bottom and top of each page, adjusting the bottom margin, if necessary, to accommodate the ending and beginning lines. Avoid single lines that carry over to end a paragraph at the top of a new page.

b. Double-space the report or manuscript. Each paragraph should be indented to offset it clearly from the previous one.

c. Number each page as follows:

(1) For pages with first-degree headings, either omit the page number or center it on the third line from the bottom of the page.

(2) For pages without first-degree headings, type the page number on the third line from the top of the page, ½ inch from the right edge of the paper.

d. Use a manuscript typing guide for setting up reports and manuscripts. Commercially prepared guides made of manila tag that indicate the remaining number of lines on a page are available. Usually these guides are larger than the standard-size paper so that the remaining number of lines are readily visible.

When commercially prepared typing guides are not available, use an 8½-by-11-inch sheet of paper to design your own. Draw heavy black lines to represent the left and right margins as well as the top and bottom margins. Allow 1-inch top and bottom margins and 1¼-inch left and right margins, unless the manuscript or report is to be bound at the left; then allow a 1½-inch left margin. Draw a heavy black horizontal line 2 inches from the top edge (to signify the location of major headings) and a vertical line directly between the left and right margins (to aid in centering). At the right edge of the paper, number the lines of the last 4 inches of paper. Separate each inch with a 1-inch horizontal line as illustrated in the example (to assist in gauging the end of the paper and in setting up footnotes). Finally, type ¼-inch lines where both the top and bottom page numbers are to be located.

typing guide

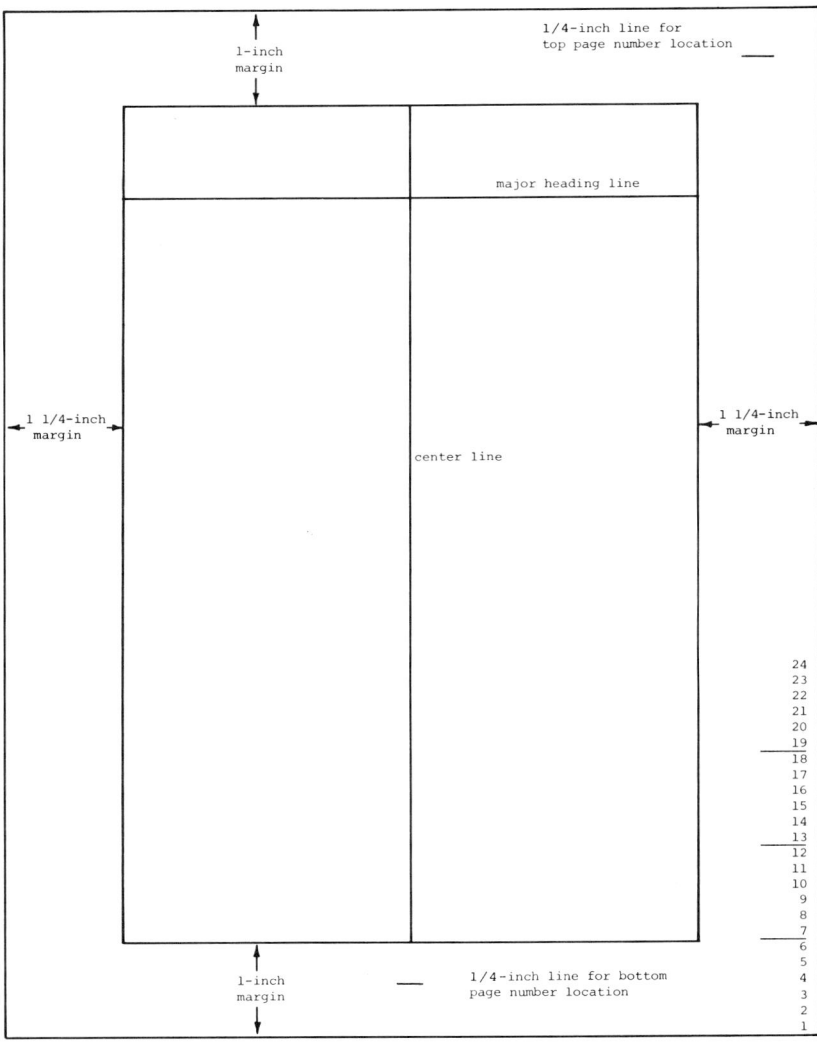

body of report

SECTION I

INTRODUCTION

The following report is a comparison of the employees' health
insurance policies submitted by eight major insurance companies.

Purpose of the Report

In January Mr. Norman Rittgers, the employees' representative for
our company, requested that health insurance be considered by the Board
of Directors as a supplement to our wage schedule. Consequently, the
board directed the Personnel Department to (1) contact insurance companies to determine what health insurance policies were available and
(2) compare the coverages to determine which policy would best meet our
employees' health needs for the least cost.

Scope of the Report

The scope of this investigation was limited to the written policies
submitted by participating insurance companies. Of the 28 insurance
companies contacted, most gave verbal explanations as to what the estimated coverage and cost of a group health insurance policy for our company employees would be. Only eight of these companies, however,
submitted written policies for our consideration. These eight policies
were then compared in several ways:

11

body of report

Company Cost Per Employee

Each health insurance package was analyzed to determine the cost
per employee to the company. This analysis took into consideration
such variables as discounts for insuring over a certain number of people and added interest for making payments on a quarterly rather than
an annual basis.

Cost to Employees

None of the health insurance packages shown in this report included
any cost to employees. Some of the policies did, however, include op-
tions whereby individual employees could increase the amount of coverage
at their own expense.

Kinds of Illnesses and/or Injuries Covered

Although all the health insurance packages shown in this report
covered most of the common types of illnesses and injuries, there were
differences in specific coverages. The most common differences appeared
in coverages for illnesses resulting in operations, and these differences
were analyzed in reaching the final recommendation.

Hospital, Out-Patient, and Home-Visit Coverages

Each health insurance package was analyzed to determine (1) hospital, out-patient, and home-visit coverages and (2) length of time for
which the patient was covered under these categories.

Dollar Amounts of Coverage

Information regarding the basic dollar amount of coverage, the
deductive amount (if any) for each family member, and the availability
of extended coverage was obtained and analyzed for each of the eight

11

11–8. Headings

Headings of different degrees are used to signal content in a report or manuscript. Type each degree heading as follows:

first-degree heading

<pre>
                              FIRST-DEGREE HEADINGS

        Place a first-degree heading 2 inches from the top edge of the page.

Center the heading and type it in all capital letters. Triple-space

after a first-degree heading.
</pre>

second-degree heading

<pre>
                              Second-Degree Headings

        A second-degree heading is centered and typed in capital and

lowercase letters. Triple-space before a second-degree heading and

double-space after it.
</pre>

third-degree heading

<pre>
        Third-Degree Headings

        Begin a third-degree heading at the left margin. Use capital and

lowercase letters with a continuous underline. Triple-space before a

third-degree heading and double-space after it.
</pre>

11

fourth-degree heading

> Fourth-degree headings. The fourth-degree heading is part of the
> paragraph that follows. Only the first word in the heading is capital-
> ized. The entire heading is underlined and followed by a period.
> Double-space before a fourth-degree heading and begin typing the
> paragraph on the same line as the heading.

11–9. Listings

Both vertical and horizontal lists are often used in letters, memos, reports, and manuscripts. A description and illustration of each type follows.

vertical lists

> Use the following format for listing items vertically:
>
> 1. Introduce a vertical listing with a complete thought.
> 2. Double-space before the first item, between items, and after the last item in the list.
> 3. Indent the listed items three to five spaces from both the left and the right margins.
> 4. Single-space items that are more than one line.
> 5. Begin the second and succeeding lines of an item directly under the first line, not under the number.
> 6. Capitalize the first word in each listed item.
> 7. Use a period after each item only in listings of complete sentences.

horizontal lists

> Use the following format for listing items horizontally: (a) use a colon
> before the list when it is preceded by a complete thought, (b) capitalize
> the first word of each item only when it is a proper noun, and (c) identify
> the listed items by enclosing either letters or numbers in parentheses.

11–10. Footnotes

a. Footnotes are used when the source of an idea, statement, or opinion is not the writer's and needs to be documented. Indicate the presence of a footnote by typing a superior (slightly raised) figure after the reference material to be documented. Type the footnote itself at the bottom of the page where the reference notation appears.

(1) Set the footnotes off from the rest of the page by typing a 1½-inch line at the left margin, single-spaced after the last line on the page. Use the underline key, and double-space after typing this line.

(2) Indent five spaces and number each footnote consecutively by typing a superior figure at the beginning of the footnote.

(3) Single-space each footnote, but double-space between footnotes.

(4) Type the name of the author, if any, in a first-name, last-name sequence.

(5) Indicate the complete title of the cited reference. Place in quotation marks the titles of magazine articles, sections of books, and newspaper columns. Underline or type in all capital letters the titles of books, magazines, and newspapers.

(6) Follow the complete title of books with the name of the publisher, its geographical location, and the date of publication. Elirninate the state name from the geographical location when the city is commonly known.

(7) Follow the complete title of magazines and newspapers with the date of publication.

(8) Conclude footnotes with reference to the page location of the cited material.

book, one author

```
        ¹Richard R. McCready, Solving Business Problems with Calculators,
5th Ed., Wadsworth Publishing Company, Belmont, California, 1977, p. 86.
```

book, two authors

```
        ²E. Bryant Phillips and Sylvia Lane, Personal Finance, 2nd Ed.,
John Wiley & Sons, Inc., New York, 1978, p. 109.
```

paperback book

```
        ³Harold J. Leavitt, Managerial Psychology, 3rd Ed., University of
Chicago Press, Chicago, 1975, pp. 26-27.
```

11

magazine article with author

> ^{4}Sanford Rose, "Multinational Corporations in a Tough New World," <u>Fortune</u>, August, 1974, pp. 52-53.

magazine article without author

> ^{5}"Electronic Calculators," <u>Changing Times</u>, July, 1979, p.40.

newspaper article with author

> ^{6}Richard A. Donnelly, "Commodities Corner," <u>Barrons</u>, August 13, 1977, p. 31, col. 5, p. 32, cols. 3-4.

government publication

> ^{7}<u>Statistical Abstract of the United States</u>, U.S. Bureau of the Census, Washington, D.C., 1978, p. 56.

b.   Once a reference has been cited, a shortened form may be used when the same reference is shown again.

> ^{2}<u>Ibid</u>. Used when the reference is identical to the one in the preceding footnote. <u>Ibid</u>. means "in the same place."
>
> ^{3}<u>Ibid</u>., pp. 14-15. Used when the reference is identical to the one in the preceding footnote except for the page numbers cited.
>
> ^{4}Donnelly, <u>loc. cit</u>. Used when the reference has been cited previously, the same page numbers are being referenced, but intervening footnotes have occurred.
>
> ^{5}Leavitt, <u>op. cit</u>., p. 74. Used when the reference has been cited previously, different page numbers are being referenced, and intervening footnotes have occurred.

11

c. References to the bibliography may be used as an alternative to formal foot-notes. The reference to the bibliography is shown in parentheses at the end of the cited material by referring first to the number of the reference in the bibliography and following this number with a colon and the page number(s) of the source.

bibliographical footnotes

. . . Income has risen 16 percent during the last fiscal period. To

offset this increased income, however, expenses have risen 21 percent

over the same period. (6:10-11)

11–11. Tables

a. Tables may be used to illustrate data described in a report. When possible, the table should appear on the same page as the narrative describing it. If there is insufficient space on the same page for the table and its explanation, then the table should be placed on the following page. A statement such as "As shown by Table 3 on page 9, . . ." should be used in the narrative to direct the reader to the illustration.

b. Although the length, number of columns, and style of tables will vary according to the type of data presented, there are some general procedures to use in setting up tables.

(1) Leave three blank lines before and after a table if it does not appear on a separate page.

(2) If more than one table appears in the report, number each table consecutively, using arabic numerals. Center *Table* and its corresponding number over the proposed position of the table.

(3) Double-space and then center under the table number the title of the table; use all capital letters. If a secondary title is needed, center and use capital and lowercase letters for this subtitle, beginning a double space below the main title. Triple-space after the final line of either the main title or subtitle.

(4) If columnar headings are used, allow a sufficient number of lines to center these headings attractively and to allow a double space between the last line of the heading and the first line of the data. After the columns have been typed, center the carriage over the longest line in each column and then back-space once for every two spaces in the column heading. Type each heading in capital and lowercase letters and underline the last line of the heading.

(5) Center tabular columns horizontally using either the back-space or arithmetic method of horizontal centering.
For the back-space method for horizontal centering:

11

235

(a)   Center the carriage halfway between the left and right margins of the report.

(b)   Determine the number of spaces to be left between columns. Leave from 4 to 12 spaces between columns, depending upon the number and length of the columns.

(c)   Back-space once for every two spaces between columns and once for every two characters and spaces in the longest line of each column (including the heading). Set the left margin of the typewriter at this point.

(d)   Set tabulator stops at the beginning of each column by spacing forward one space for each character and space in the longest line of each column and once for each space to be left between the columns.

For the arithmetic method for horizontal centering:

(a)   Count the number of characters and spaces in the longest line of each column (including the heading) plus the total number of spaces to be left between the columns.

(b)   Divide the total of step (a) by two. Subtract this number from the center point of the typewriter (51 for elite and 43 for pica). Set the left margin of the typewriter at this point.

(c)   Set tabulator stops at the beginning of each column by spacing forward one space for each character and space in the longest line in each column and once for each space to be left between the columns.

(6)   A table appearing on a separate page should be centered vertically as well as horizontally.

(a)   Count the number of lines and the spaces between the lines to be used in the table.

(b)   Subtract the total number of lines and spaces from 66 (the number of lines on standard, 11-inch typing paper).

(c)   Divide the difference obtained in step (b) by two. The result is the number of blank lines between the top edge of the paper and the table number.

a table

Table 1

A COMPARISON OF THE ANNUAL COST PER EMPLOYEE
OF HEALTH INSURANCE POLICIES
SUBMITTED BY EIGHT COMPANIES

March 1, 1980

Company	Plan A[1]	Plan B[2]	Plan C[3]
Chicago General	$375.00	$492.50	$545.00
Concord	325.00	450.00	510.00
D & P Life	385.50	485.50	585.50
Edgewater	312.50	443.50	513.50
Lincoln	415.00	500.00	655.00
Morgan	309.34	440.25	524.15
New Jersey	350.00	475.00	530.00
Western	405.60	595.00	620.30

[1] $10,000 maximum annual coverage
[2] $15,000 maximum annual coverage
[3] $20,000 maximum annual coverage

Bibliography

11–12. Content

The bibliography follows immediately after the body of the report or manuscript and contains all footnoted sources. Any source material that is not footnoted but that has contributed directly to the development of a report or manuscript should also be included.

11–13. Format

List the items in the bibliography alphabetically by authors' last names. Consecutively number each item in the bibliography if the informal form of footnoting is used.

(1) Type the heading *Bibliography* in first-degree form.

(2) Triple-space between the heading and the first reference.

(3) Single-space each reference and double-space between references. If a reference requires more than one line, indent the second and succeeding lines five spaces.

(4) If an author has more than one reference listed, type a five-space line in place of his name, starting with the second reference.

(5) When the author is unknown, alphabetize the references by title.

(6) End the references for magazines, journals, or other multisource articles with page references. For books, conclude the reference with the number of pages in the publication.

newspaper column with author

```
                          BIBLIOGRAPHY

Donnelly, Richard A., "Commodities Corner," Barrons, August 13, 1977.
     pp. 31-32.
```

magazine article with author

```
     Rose, Sanford, "Multinational Corporations in a Tough New World,"
          Fortune, August, 1974, pp. 52-56.
```

magazine article without author

```
     "Electronic Calculators," Changing Times, July, 1979, pp. 39-41.
```

237

article in professional journal

> Humphrey, Susan R. and Gerald F. Williamson, "Make Your Technical
> Reports 'People Oriented,'" <u>American Business Communication
> Association Bulletin</u>, 35, December, 1971, pp. 27-31.

paperback book

> Leavitt, Harold J., <u>Managerial Psychology</u>, 3rd Ed., University of
> Chicago Press, Chicago, 1975, 434 pp.

book, one author

> McCready, Richard R., <u>Solving Business Problems With Calculators</u>,
> 5th Ed., Wadsworth Publishing Company, Belmont, California, 1977,
> 278 pp.

book, same author

> _____, <u>Business Mathematics</u>, 3rd Ed., Wadsworth Publishing
> Company, Belmont, California, 1978, 314 pp.

book, two authors

> Phillips, E. Bryant and Sylvia Lane, <u>Personal Finance</u>, 2nd Ed., John
> Wiley & Sons, Inc., New York, 1978, 536 pp.

government publication

> <u>Statistical Abstract of the United States</u>, U.S. Bureau of the Census,
> Washington, D.C., 1978, 973 pp.

11 Appendix

11–14. Content

The appendix follows the bibliography and contains material of a supportive nature. This material may include such items as letters, copies of questionnaires, maps, contracts, lists, tables, and other documents not shown elsewhere.

11–15. Format

The appendix may be preceded by a page entitled *Appendix* (typed in all capital letters and centered both horizontally and vertically). This introductory page may also include a list of the items included in the appendix. In this case, both the title and the listing are centered vertically or the title may be typed 2 inches from the top edge of the page with the listing beginning a triple space thereafter. The material may be numbered with alphabetic letters if more than one item appears in the appendix.

introductory appendix page

```
                                    APPENDIXES


             Appendix A:  Copy of the initial letter from the employees'
                          representative requesting health insurance
                          coverage

             Appendix B:  Copies of the eight health insurance policies
                          submitted
```

12

mail, telegrams, and cablegrams

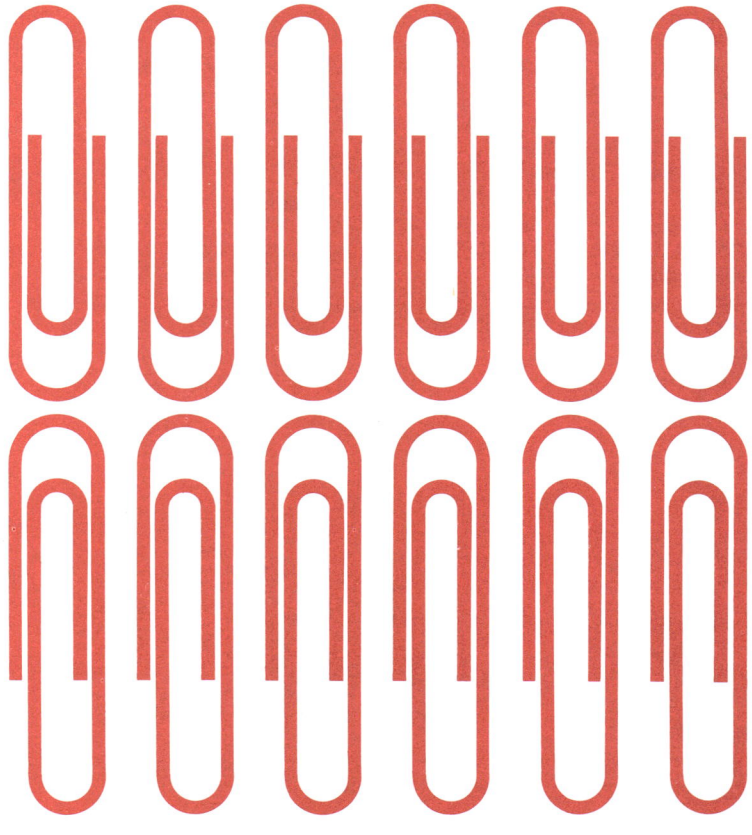

Mail, Telegrams, and Cablegrams Solution Finder

12

Domestic Mail Classes and Services

There are a number of mail classes and services. Each varies in (1) the type, weight, and size of the matter that may be sent; (2) the cost of mailing; and (3) the priority in which the mail will be delivered.

12–1. Express Mail Service

Express mail receives the highest priority handling in terms of destination arrival time. It is a high-speed, intercity delivery system geared to the special needs of business and industry for the fast transfer of letters, documents, or merchandise. All domestic shipments sent by express mail are insured against loss or damage at no extra charge.

a. *Express mail next-day service* is available only in major cities throughout the United States, and each city has its list of other cities to which it guarantees this service. Express mail may be sent post office to post office or post office to addressee. This means that mail brought in by 5 p.m. will be delivered to its destination post office by 10 a.m. or to the addressee by 3 p.m. the following day.

b. *Express mail same-day airport service* provides service between major airports within the United States. Items dispatched are sent on the first available flight to the destination airport, to be picked up by the addressee upon arrival.

12–2. First Class Mail

The following examples are always considered first class mail if the weight is 13 ounces or less:

(1) Handwritten and typewritten messages, including identical copies, but excluding computer material

(2) Bills and statements of account

(3) Notebooks or account books containing handwritten or typewritten entries

(4) Postcards and postal cards

(5) Canceled and uncanceled checks

(6) Printed forms filled out in writing

(7) Printed price lists with written or typed changes

(8) Greeting cards, sealed and not marked "Third Class"

(9) Business reply mail

(10) Any other type of mail weighing 13 ounces or less sent as first class at the option of the mailer

12

For oversized materials (larger than legal-size envelopes), use the white envelopes with a green diamond border. This border automatically indicates that these materials are to be sent first class.

a. *Priority mail* is first class mail weighing over 13 ounces. The rate schedule is determined by weight and zone, but the delivery time is faster than for fourth class mail. The maximum weight for priority mail is 70 pounds, and its dimensions are limited to 100 inches in length and girth combined.

b. *Business reply mail* is a first class mail service supplied to mailers who want to encourage responses by paying the postage. The mailer guarantees that he will pay the postage plus a fee for all replies returned to him.

c. *Mailgram service* provides next-business-day delivery for messages to addressees in the United States and Canada. By taking directly or telephoning in a message to a Western Union office, the sender can ensure delivery with the next business day's mail. The message is transmitted electronically to a post office near its destination from where it is placed in a special envelope and delivered with regular mail.

12–3. Second Class Mail

Second class mail is used primarily by newspaper and magazine publishers to mail publications at a special bulk rate. A publisher mails at the second class rate on the basis of a permit obtained from the post office.

Publications must be issued at least four times annually to qualify for the special bulk rate. The regular second class postage rate varies depending upon the frequency of publication, the advertising portion of the publication's content, and whether or not the publication is mailed to an address within the county of publication.

A mailer other than a publisher can mail individual, complete copies of a publication by paying what is called a "transient rate." This mail should be marked "Second Class."

12–4. Third Class Mail

Third class mail consists of circulars, booklets, catalogs, and other printed materials such as newsletters or proof sheets. It also includes merchandise, farm and factory products, photographs, keys, and printed drawings.

Each piece of third class mail is limited in weight to fewer than 16 ounces. The same material weighing 16 ounces or more is classified as fourth class, or parcel post, mail.

12

Third class mail may be sent at a single-piece rate or at a bulk rate. Additionally, certain nonprofit organizations qualify for a special third class bulk postage rate. Keys and identification devices may be mailed for still another rate.

12–5. Fourth Class Mail (Parcel Post)

Fourth class mail is generally called "parcel post." Size and weight restrictions vary according to the post office from which mail is sent and the one to which it is addressed. Some post offices restrict weight to 40 pounds and combined length and girth to 84 inches. Others restrict weight to a maximum of 70 pounds and combined length and girth to 100 inches. The minimum weight for fourth class mail is 16 ounces per item; mail under this weight is sent at third class rates. Parcel post postage rates are determined by the weight of the parcel and the distance from its point of origin to its destination.

a. A *bulk rate fourth class mail* is available for sending 300 or more pieces that are identical in weight.

b. A *special fourth class rate* may be used for mailing books, certain kinds of films, printed music, printed test materials, sound recordings, play scripts, manuscripts, educational reference charts, and medical information. Books containing advertising for merchandise, telephone directories, corporation reports, house organs, and periodicals do not qualify for this special rate.

All items mailed with the *special fourth class rate* should be marked as such. In addition, note a description of the item, such as "Books," "Sound Recordings," "Films," etc.

c. *Library rate* is used for certain kinds of materials that are loaned, exchanged between, or mailed by or to schools, colleges, libraries, museums, or certain nonprofit organizations. Materials include books, printed music, academic theses, sound recordings, etc. All items must be marked "Library Rate."

d. Securely bound advertising, promotional, directory, or educational material may be sent at a special *bound printed matter* rate. Material may not have the nature of personal correspondence and cannot be a book.

12–6. Mixed Classes

A first class letter may be attached to or enclosed in a parcel sent by a lower class. If the letter is attached to the parcel, each item should have separate postage. If the letter is enclosed in the package, "First Class Mail Enclosed" should be marked on the outside of the parcel, along with the correct postage for both items.

12–7. Special Delivery

This special service is used to hasten the delivery of a mailed item. Special delivery means an item of mail is delivered *as soon as practicable* after it arrives at the addressee's post office. It virtually assures delivery on the working day received at that post office but does not necessarily speed up the transportation time to that point from its origin. All classes of mail may be sent special delivery for an additional fee.

12

12-8. Special Handling

A special handling service is provided for preferential handling in the dispatch and transportation of third and fourth class mail. A special handling fee must be paid on parcels that take special care, such as baby chicks, baby alligators, etc.

12-9. Insured Mail

a. *Registered mail* may be used only for domestic first class, priority mail, or c.o.d. parcels, with each mailing insured for its full value up to $10,000. This service is offered for the protection of valuable papers, jewelry, and other items of value. Registered mail may not be deposited in collection boxes since a receipt must be issued at the point of mailing.

The registry fees, in addition to first class or priority mail postage, are scaled according to the declared value of the mail. For an additional fee, one can obtain a proof of delivery receipt and/or restrict to whom the mail is delivered.

b. *Insured mail* consists of third and fourth class mail items insured for protection against loss or damage. Official government mail bearing "Postage and Fees Paid" may also be insured. Priority mail containing third or fourth class matter may be insured provided it bears the endorsement "Contains Third Class (or Fourth Class) Mail."

Unnumbered or minimum fee insured mail is delivered as ordinary parcel mail, and the limit of indemnity is $15. Numbered insured mail insures mail valued at over $15, with a maximum indemnity of $200. A receipt is given to the mailer at the time of mailing, and a signature is required upon delivery. For insured mail of more than $15 declared value, a return receipt and/or restricted delivery can be requested.

c. *COD* (collect on delivery) may be used for first, third, and fourth class mail. When the mail is delivered, the addressee pays the amount due for the contents. The addressee may also be required to pay the postage and the c.o.d. fee, depending upon the prior agreement between the sender and receiver.

The c.o.d. fee includes insurance against loss, damage, or failure to receive the amount collected from the addressee. The maximum amount that can be collected for one item is $300. The goods shipped must have been ordered by the addressee, and the sender agrees to pay any return postage unless specified differently on the mail.

Senders of c.o.d. mail may (1) request restricted delivery, (2) alter the charges or direct delivery to a different address, or (3) register first class mail.

d. *Postal money orders* provide for sending money through the mail safely. If they are lost or stolen, they can be replaced. Domestic money orders up to $300 may be purchased and redeemed at any post office.

12

12-10. Proof of Mailing and Delivery

There are three ways in which proof may be obtained that an item has been mailed or received.

a. *Certified mail* is used for first class and priority mail items that have no money value since there is no insurance feature with this service. Certified mail provides for a record of delivery to be maintained by the post office from which the item was delivered. The carrier delivering certified mail obtains a signature from the addressee on a receipt form that is kept for two years. In this way the sender can prove that items were received by the addressee. Proof of delivery may be obtained at a later time during the two-year period.

Return receipts showing to whom, when, and where the item was delivered may be obtained for an additional charge for mail that is registered, insured, certified, or sent c.o.d. Proof of delivery may be obtained at a later time during the two-year period.

Certified mail may be deposited in a collection box if the mailer has attached a "Certified" sticker and the appropriate postage and fees.

b. A *certificate of mailing* for any item may be obtained from the sender's post office. Unlike certified mail, however, the post office does not keep any record of the certificate issued or of the delivery of the item. It only provides proof that the item was mailed.

12–11. United Parcel Service

United Parcel Service (commonly called UPS) is a commercial company that is widely used throughout the United States to deliver small packages. Packages may be sent either by truck or by air, and customers may either take their packages to their local UPS office or have UPS pick up the packages at their home or place of business for a small extra charge. Packages sent by UPS may not weigh over 50 pounds or be over 108 inches in length and girth combined. All packages are automatically insured for up to $100.

Telegrams

12–12. Classes of Telegrams

There are three classes of telegrams. Each class varies as to speed of delivery and cost.

a. *Regular telegrams* have first priority over other telegrams and are sent immediately upon receipt, whether day or night. There is a base charge for up to 15 words, which does not include the inside address and the sender's name and title. There is an additional charge for each word in the message over the 15-word base. The local Western Union office will telephone the message to the recipient unless the sender pays an extra charge to have it delivered.

b. *Overnight telegrams* (often called night letters) can be sent at any time up until midnight and will be delivered the next morning. There is a base charge for up to 100 words. There is an additional charge for each word over the 100-word base. The local Western Union office will telephone the message to the recipient unless the sender pays an extra charge to have it delivered.

12

c. *Mailgrams* are sent by Western Union to the local post office of the addressee. The message is then delivered by regular mail. There is a base charge for up to 100 words and an additional charge for each 100 words or less over this base.

12–13. Sending Telegrams

Although telegraph messages that are telephoned to a Western Union office will be accepted, the chance of the message being misunderstood can be lessened if the message is typed on either an official telegraph form or on regular paper and delivered to the telegraph office. Official telegraph forms can be readily obtained at any Western Union office. The following are some suggestions in preparing telegraph messages.

a. Use only those words that are necessary to make the message clear. Unnecessary words such as *I, you, the, a, and,* etc., should be omitted. For example, it is better to write, "Arriving United Flight 424 LAX 8 p.m., Jan 24. Please meet.," than "I will arrive on United Flight 424 at Los Angeles International Airport at 8 p.m. on Friday, January 24. I would appreciate your meeting me."

b. The wording of a telegram is charged as follows:

(1) Regular words used in a standard dictionary are counted as one word regardless of length. Other words are counted as one word for every five letters.

(2) Proper names are counted as they are written (New Mexico, 2 words; Van Der Meter, 3 words).

(3) Abbreviations, code words, and groups of figures are counted as one word for each five characters.

(4) Punctuation marks are not counted.

Cablegrams

Cablegrams are similar to telegrams, except they are sent outside the continental United States.

12–14. Classes of Cablegrams

a. *Full rate* is the fastest and, consequently, the most expensive type of cablegram. Either ordinary words, coded words, or a combination of the two may be used. There is a base charge for up to 7 words, but there is no charge for specifying that the cablegram is to be sent full rate (FR).

b. *Letter rate* cablegrams are normally delivered the day after they are sent. There is a base charge for up to 22 words, including the letter rate symbol (LR), which is counted as one word. Only ordinary words may be used at this rate.

12

12–15. Charges for Cablegrams

The wording of a cablegram is charged as follows:

(1)   A word of 15 letters counts as two words.

(2)   Each word in the address counts as one word except for the name of the country where the cablegram is to be sent.

(3)   Each word in the signature counts as one word.

(4)   Initials with spaces between are counted as separate words.

(5)   Abbreviations, code words, and groups of figures are counted as one word for each five characters.

12

appendix
secretarial shortcuts

A

Secretarial Shortcuts Solution Finder

Simplified Typing Practices

A–1. Placement Guides

a. Use a letter placement guide for setting up correspondence. Place the guide directly behind the original but in front of any carbon copies. The lines on the guide will assist you in setting margins, placing the date, and calculating the letter length. Make your own guide on 8½-by-11-inch paper by following the specifications on the sample guide.

The heavy horizontal line at the top of the guide signifies the location of the date for standard-depth letterhead stationery. Should the letterhead drop farther, type the date a double space below the last line of the letterhead.

The outermost group of lines represents the parameters of a long letter (200 or more words); the middle group of lines represents the parameters of a medium-length letter (100 to 200 words); and the innermost group of lines represents the parameters of a short letter (fewer than 100 words). Estimate the length of your letter and set the left margin at the corresponding line. For the right side, set the margin five spaces to the right of the appropriate line to allow for the typewriter warning bell.

The numbers at the right edge of the placement guide indicate the number of standard typewritten lines remaining on the page. These numbers may be used to assist in determining whether the closing lines should be expanded or condensed so that a balanced placement can be achieved. The line indicators will also be useful for typing two-page letters by showing the remaining number of lines on the page.

The letter placement guide may be altered to accommodate other than standard-size stationery and standard-spacing typewriters.

A

letter placement guide

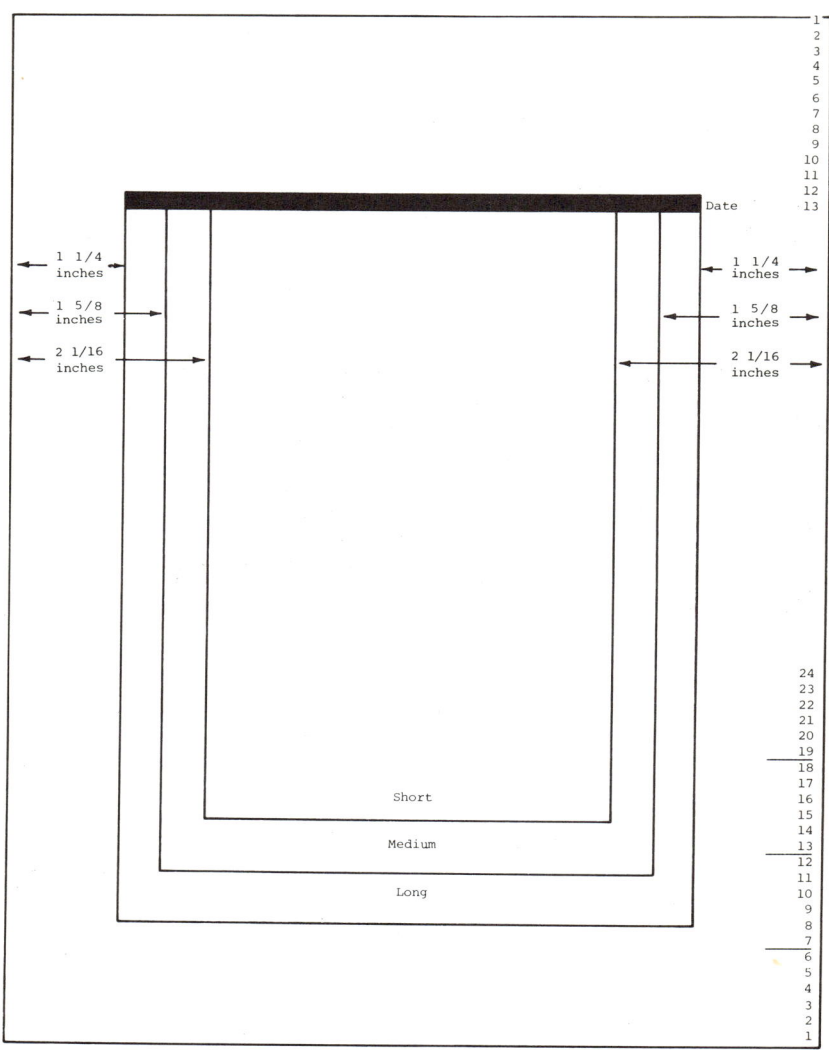

b. Use a manuscript typing guide for setting up reports and manuscripts. Commercially prepared guides made of manila tag that indicate the remaining number of lines on a page are available. Usually these guides are larger than the standard-size paper so that the remaining number of lines is readily visible.

When commercially prepared typing guides are not available, use an 8½-by-11-inch sheet of paper to design your own. Draw heavy black lines to represent the left and right margins as well as the top and bottom margins. Allow 1-inch

A

top and bottom margins and 1¼-inch left and right margins, unless the manuscript or report is to be bound at the left; then allow a 1½-inch left margin. Draw
a heavy black horizontal line 2 inches from the top edge (to signify the location
of major headings) and a vertical line directly between the left and right margins
(to aid in centering). At the right edge of the paper, number the lines of the last 4
inches of paper. Separate each inch with a 1-inch horizontal line (to assist in
gauging the end of the paper and in setting up footnotes). Finally, type ¼-inch
lines where both the top and bottom page numbers are to be located. An
illustration of this guide is shown on page 228.

commercial typing guide

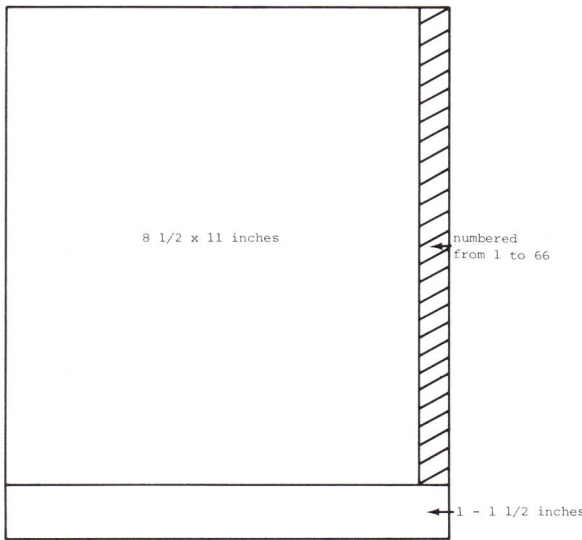

c. Use page-ending strips to calculate page endings when placement guides or
typewriters with page-ending devices are not available. Using your typewriter,
number vertically from 1 to 10 on a 1-inch strip of paper. (Initially use a larger
piece of paper and cut it to size.) Fasten the strip to the left side of your
typewriter platen with transparent tape. Align all papers to be typed with the
numeral 1. After typing the first page, note the numeral on which your work
concludes, and end all succeeding pages at this numeral.

d. When you type tabulations requiring spacing identical to that of a previously
typed report, use a horizontal and vertical measurement ruler that measures
spacing for both elite and pica typewriters. By placing the ruler on the previously
typed report, you can determine where margins and tabulator stops were set
and the number of blank lines between typewritten lines.

A

A–2. Multiple Copies

a. Use photocopying equipment when two or more copies are required. The time saved in preparing camera-ready copy not requiring multiple corrections makes up for the cost of photocopies.

b. When photocopying equipment is not available for making multiple copies, use carbon packs. Place a backing sheet of manila tag behind the last sheet to prevent the carbon paper from wrinkling and printing "trees" on your copies. Should trees still result after using the backing sheet, have the typewriter re-pairman check your platen.

c. To keep multiple carbons in alignment when inserting a carbon pack into the typewriter, place a folded half sheet of paper at the top of the pack.

Turn the carbon pack so that the top edge is at the bottom, with the last carbon or backing sheet facing you.

Insert the carbon pack into the typewriter so that the folded edge of the half sheet enters the typewriter first. Upon insertion, remove the half sheet of paper. Your carbon pack should have retained its alignment.

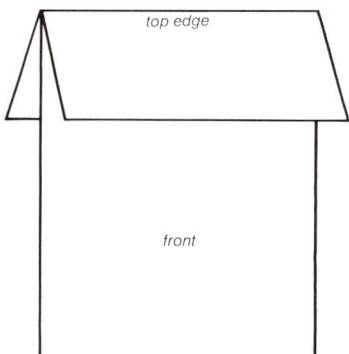
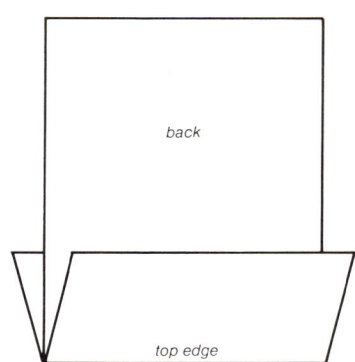

d. Occasionally it is necessary to use extra large carbon packs that will not readily be accepted by the typewriter platen. In these cases, use an old file folder to feed the carbon pack into the typewriter. Cut the folder according to the diagram.

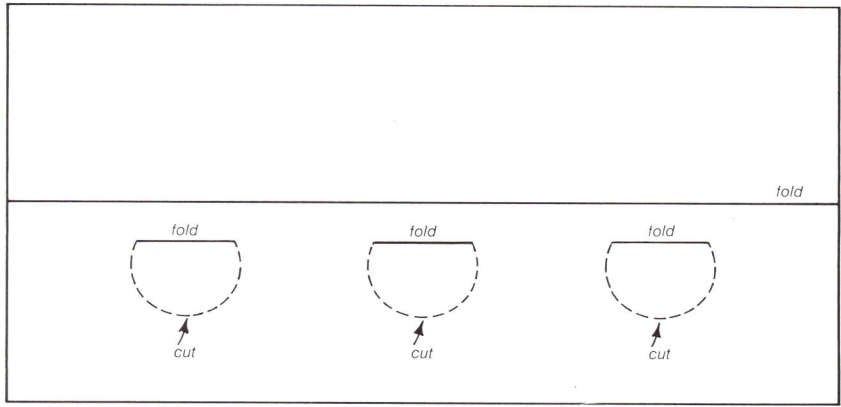

Place the top edge of the carbon pack in the center fold with the back of the carbon pack facing you.

Insert the carbon pack into the typewriter by first allowing the platen to grip the cut-outs from the slots in the folded strip. Once the platen grasps the cut-outs, the carbon pack may be rolled in smoothly. Remove the folded strip after inserting the carbon pack.

A–3. Typewritten Corrections

a. When possible, simplify corrections by using an opaquing fluid or correction tape to block out errors. Such a procedure is faster than erasing. For quality

A

results be sure the color of the fluid or tape matches closely the color of the stationery you are using.

When using opaquing fluid or correction tape, make additional copies on a photocopy machine. If carbon copies are preferred, however, corrections may be made in the following manner. When using correction tape, insert an eraser guard between the original and the carbon. Retype the error on the original. Remove the eraser guard and type the correct letter. Use a fine surgical blade to remove the incorrect carbon deposits on the carbon copies.

An alternate procedure for correcting carbon-copy errors is to use a special copy correction tape simultaneously with the correction tape for originals. Sheets are inserted before each copy; the incorrect letter is typed; the sheets are removed; and the correct character is then imposed where the previous letter was blocked out.

When using opaquing fluid for correcting originals that require additional copies, type the correct letter over the opaqued area, allowing the letter to print on the carbon copies. Remove incorrect imprints from the copies with a fine surgical blade.

b. To erase smoothly, use a soft eraser, a hard eraser, and a small brush. On standard-carriage typewriters, move the carriage to the extreme right or left so that eraser or paper crumbs will not fall into the type basket. Begin erasing by removing the excess ink with the soft eraser. Remove the embedded ink with the hard eraser, and smooth out the surface with the soft eraser. Be sure to brush away all eraser crumbs before continuing to type. When carbon copies are involved, insert an eraser guard behind each copy as you erase so that the carbon copies will not become smudged by the erasing strokes.

Corrections on erased carbons are often fainter than the remainder of the type. To avoid this occurrence, place the ribbon position on stencil after making the correction. Type the correct letter once. Then return the ribbon to its regular position and type the letter again. In this way, the density of the carbon copy correction will be increased while not affecting the density of the correction on the original.

c. Keep your eraser clean by affixing a piece of fine sandpaper to the side of your typewriter with transparent tape. Then, when black marks appear on your eraser, you can remove them by rubbing your eraser against the sandpaper.

d. Make corrections at the bottom edge of the paper by releasing the ratchet and feeding back the paper until the error is free of the platen. Erase, return the page to the original position, and secure the ratchet. You are now ready to continue typing.

e. If a correction must be made after work has been removed from the typewriter, make corrections on each sheet individually. To align the work properly, use your paper release and align a straight letter (*i* or *l*) with one of the markings on the typewriter scale. Move your ribbon position to stencil and type the correct letter. A faint outline will allow you to determine whether or not you have achieved the proper placement. You may then return your ribbon to its typing position and strike the letter again.

A

If your typewriter does not have a carbon ribbon, be sure your correction key is clean by typing the character several times on a scrap piece of paper. Residual ink on the typewriter key may leave an imprint, even though the ribbon is in stencil position.

f. To make corrections in top-bound manuscripts, first remove the error. Then insert a sheet of paper in the typewriter, advancing the platen until the paper protrudes about 1 inch above the typing scale. Between the paper and the platen at the front of the machine, place the bottom edge of the page to be corrected. Next, reverse the platen until the typewriter grips the sheet. Use the procedure described in A–3e to align the work and make the correction.

A–4. Cards and Labels

a. Continuous-feed labels provide the most efficient means for typing labels because they may be easily inserted into the typewriter. When single labels or small cards must be inserted into the machine, however, slippage may occur. To solve this problem, use a pleat sheet to hold the label or card.

Fold a horizontal pleat approximately ¼ inch in diameter in the middle of a standard sheet of paper. Use the following procedures to make the pleat.

(1) Fold sheet in half.

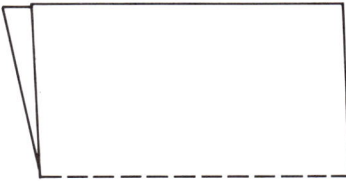

(2) Lay the sheet flat so that the folded side faces away from you.

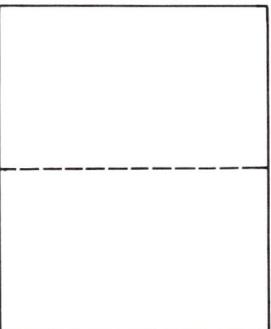

A

(3) Bring up the bottom edge ½ inch below the top edge and fold.

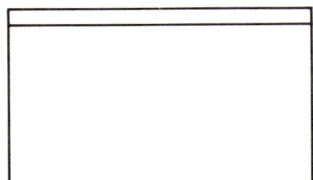

(4) Arrange in fanfold and crease with ruler to form a pocket. Tape back side of pocket with transparent tape.

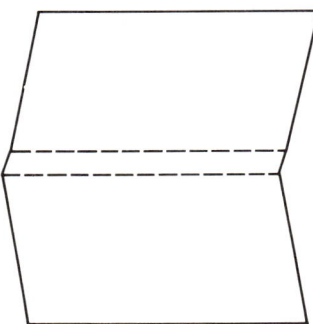

Release the ratchet and roll the sheet into the platen until the fold reaches the edge of the typewriter scale. Insert the label or card into the fold. Then roll back the platen to the desired writing line and secure your ratchet. The pleat will hold the card or label while you type the needed information.

b. Small cards may be chain fed by feeding the cards from the front of your typewriter. Type the first card in the usual manner. Then roll the card back until just ¼ to ½ inch of the card protrudes above the typewriter scale. Insert the next card at the front of your typewriter by placing the bottom edge of the card between the first card and the platen. Reverse your platen until the card is in position to type. Continue feeding succeeding cards in the same manner. Completed cards will stack neatly on the paper table of your typewriter.

A–5. Chain Feeding Envelopes

a. To chain feed envelopes from the front of your typewriter, insert an envelope in the usual manner and type the address. Roll back the envelope until ½ inch of the top edge protrudes above the typewriter scale. Between the first envelope and the platen, insert the bottom edge of the next envelope. Reverse the platen until you reach the appropriate typing line. Type the address and then reverse the platen until ½ inch of the top edge of the envelope protrudes above the typewriter scale. Continue with these insertion and typing procedures until all

A

the envelopes have been addressed. Envelopes will stack neatly on the paper table of your typewriter.

b. For unusually thick envelopes, chain feed from the back of the typewriter. Insert an envelope, with its flap extended, into the typewriter. Roll the platen forward until the top edge of the envelope (the crease between the flap and the envelope) reaches the typewriter scale. With its flap extended, insert another envelope at the back of the typewriter between the first envelope and the platen. Advance the platen to the appropriate writing line on the first envelope and type the address. Again move the platen forward until the bottom edge of the first envelope is released from the typewriter. Then, between the second envelope and the platen, insert into the back of the typewriter another envelope with its flap extended. Advance the platen and type the address on the second envelope. Again, move the platen forward until the bottom edge of the second envelope is released from the typewriter. Insert another envelope with its flap extended into the back of the typewriter between the third envelope and the platen. Continue the above procedure until all envelopes have been addressed.

A–6. Drawing Lines on the Typewriter

a. When possible, use the automatic underscore on the electric typewriter to draw both horizontal and vertical lines. On typewriters with long carriages, reverse the position of your work and use the automatic underscore key to type vertical lines.

b. To draw horizontal lines with a pen or pencil, insert the writing instrument in the special cut-out on the typewriter scale or in the fork of the ribbon guide. Advance the pen or pencil across the page with the carriage release lever. For stationary-carriage typewriters, advance the machine with the tabulator mechanism, setting tabulator stops at the beginning and end of the horizontal lines. Practice this procedure several times before using it.

c. To draw vertical lines, insert the writing instrument in the special cut-out on the typewriter scale or in the fork of the ribbon guide. Position the carriage where the vertical line is to be drawn and release the ratchet. While holding the pen or pencil firmly, advance the platen to draw the line.

A–7. Blind Copies

a. To type on carbon copies only, place a piece of paper over the original and over those carbon copies on which you do not wish the typing to appear. Then type the material.

b. When you wish to type on all copies except the original, remove the original from the typewriter. Position the carriage where you wish to begin typing. Then, disengage the paper release lever and *carefully* remove the original from the typewriter while firmly positioning the carbon pack. Return the paper release lever to the lock position and begin typing.

Secretarial Procedures

A–8. Follow-Up Files

Ordering priorities and meeting deadlines are the most important tasks of the administrative secretary. Consequently, an appropriate follow-up file should be part of every office operation.

a. The most common follow-up file is one that employs a file-drawer and file-folder system. Number 31 letter-size folders from 1 to 31. Label additional folders for each month of the year.

Arrange the folders in your file so that the current month and date appear first. Other folders should be arranged in chronological order with those folders representing nonworking days reversed in the file. Noncurrent month folders are placed in the back of the file until needed.

The purpose of a follow-up file is to aid in ordering priorities, meeting deadlines, and serving as a reminder to follow up on previously initiated activities. To use the file effectively, place a reminder notation under the appropriate date for all future activities. The reminder notation may take the form of a note, an *additional* carbon copy of a letter or order, or a photocopy of correspondence received. Use additional copies or make notations on separate sheets of paper for your follow-up file. Documents may be needed intermittently and may not be located easily in the follow-up file. Consequently, place the originating paperwork in its appropriate place in the regular files.

Each day consult the follow-up file to determine what action must be taken on the materials contained in that day's folder. Complete the action or file the material for action at a future date.

b. A follow-up card system is another method of maintaining a follow-up file. Instead of using folders that contain copies of documents, notations are made on 3-by-5-inch cards to act as reminders of work to be completed by a specific date.

Individual guides are numbered from 1 to 31 and others are labeled with the months of the year. Arranged in a manner identical to the folders in the follow-up file, the card system functions in a similar manner. All items requiring future action are noted on 3-by-5-inch cards and filed under the date on which they are to be completed. A daily consultation of the file enables one to keep up to date with the flow of office activities.

A–9. Filing Procedures

a. File all correspondence and other office papers in reverse chronological order. Do the same in ordering materials in notebooks or binders. More recent data are likely to be consulted first. Consequently, filing in reverse chronological order saves time by not requiring one to thumb through materials unnecessarily before locating a needed document.

follow-up file

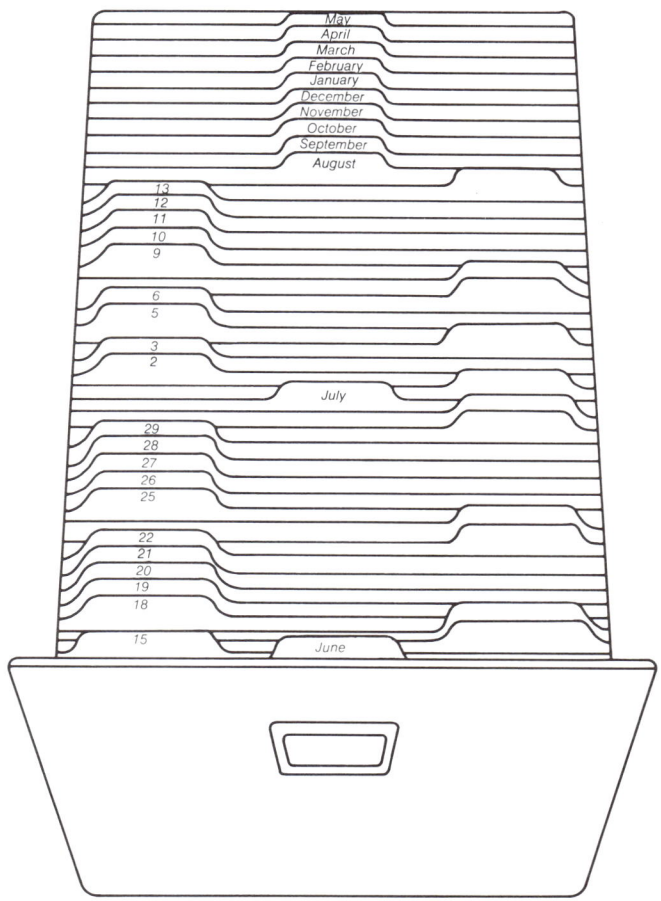

b. When active folders are removed from the files, use "out folders" instead of "out cards." Label the out folder with the usual information—the date the file was checked out, the name of the file, the name and department of the person checking out the file, and the date the file was returned.

The advantage of an out folder over an out card is that materials received subsequent to the file being checked out may be placed in the out folder until the original file is returned. In this way, important papers will not be lost or destroyed.

c. To save filing space, use the back of originating correspondence for typing a carbon to answer routine correspondence. Then only one sheet of paper will be placed in the files.

A

263

For two-page letters, use both sides of the carbon copy in making file copies. This procedure also eliminates placing an additional sheet of paper in the files.

d. When stapling materials to be placed in the files, staple the sheets on the right instead of the left side. Then other papers cannot accidentally be slipped between the stapled materials.

e. Use different colored file labels to differentiate filing systems or separate sections of a filing system. The use of colored labels will prevent misfiling and will allow materials to be located more easily.

f. Special containers are available for the filing and storage of records media used with word processing equipment. Magnetic cards, floppy disks, power typing and dictation cassettes, and diskettes may all be filed and later retrieved for use. Various configurations may be used for filing each type of media. All media may be stored with hard copy in some type of letter- or legal-size folder or binder. Other storage methods include plastic boxes, vinyl storage cases, revolving storage racks, specially designed storage pockets, etc. Each of these storage methods provides a comprehensive indexing system so that information may be located quickly. There are several different manufacturers of such filing systems. The system selected should be the one that best meets the word processing needs of the specific organization.

A–10. Color Distinctions

a. Use different colored shorthand notebooks for logging different items, taking dictation from different dictators, or for distinguishing among different time periods. Shorthand notebooks may be purchased with green, yellow, blue, pink, violet, or standard white or green-tinted paper.

b. For ease of reference, color code sections of duplicated reports by using different colored paper. This technique is especially helpful when many people must make frequent use of different sections of the materials.

c. Color code memos originating from various internal departments within the organization. Such a device distinguishes easily the originating source and enables papers to be located more easily.

d. Differentiate forms similar in size and content by printing the forms on different colored papers. Similarly, in snap-out carbon pack forms, use a different color for each copy to assist in routing the proper form to its appropriate source.

A–11. Time Savers

a. In large open offices number the desks to simplify the routing of work, the delivery of mail and supplies, the repair of typewriters, and the conducting of general office activities. Persons may be more easily directed to a desk number than to the desk of "Mary Jones" or "Larry Smith."

b. Keep an extra shorthand pad and pen in your employer's office so that you do not have to return to your desk should you be asked to take dictation when in your employer's office for another purpose.

c.   To seal a group of envelopes rapidly, layer them on your desk with the flaps open and facing you.

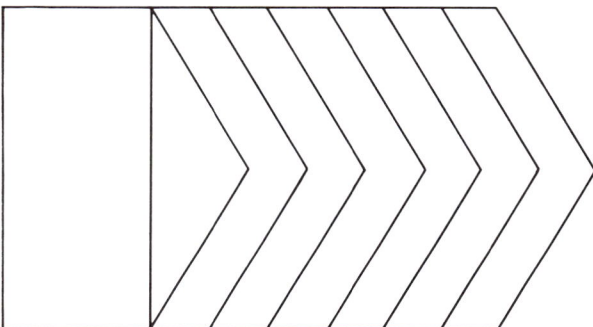

Using a sponge, moisten each flap with your right hand and then press the flap closed with your left hand. Rapidly work through the group of envelopes, moistening them with one hand and sealing and stacking them with the other.

d.   To place stamps on a group of envelopes, use stamp strips. Layer the envelopes across your desk so that the position for the stamp is visible.

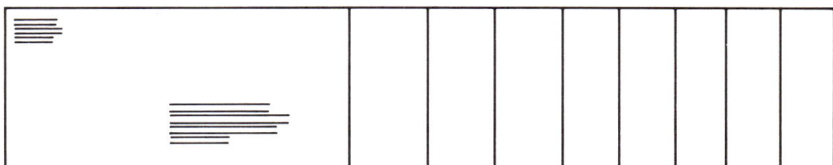

Moisten several stamps with a sponge applicator. Press the first stamp in position with your left hand. With your right hand tear the remaining stamps from the affixed one. Continue this procedure until all the envelopes have been stamped.

e.   Eliminate stuffing envelopes by using a postal card instead of a letter where possible. Economize on time, supplies, and postage in this manner.

f.   Place alphabetical index labels on your telephone book if it is consulted frequently. Index labels save time in locating names and numbers.

g.   When collating large projects, use rubber fingers to assist you in grasping the paper more easily and rapidly.

h.   Word processing equipment is ideal for storing information that must be used repetitively—namely, address lists, form letters, paragraphs, etc. This process saves time because once the information is recorded and stored in the memory, it can be accessed and used repeatedly.

iNdEX